Reckless

Reckless

THE POLITICAL ASSAULT ON THE AMERICAN ENVIRONMENT

Bob Deans

ROWMAN & LITTLEFIELD PUBLISHERS, INC.
Lanham • Boulder • New York • Toronto • Plymouth, UK

Published by Rowman & Littlefield Publishers, Inc.
A wholly owned subsidiary of The Rowman & Littlefield Publishing Group, Inc.
4501 Forbes Boulevard, Suite 200, Lanham, Maryland 20706
www.rowman.com

10 Thornbury Road, Plymouth PL6 7PP, United Kingdom

**Library of Congress Cataloging-in-Publication Data available
upon request**

978-1-4422-1797-3 (pbk: alk paper)
978-1-4422-1798-0 (electronic

∞™ The paper used in this publication meets the minimum requirements
of American National Standard for Information Sciences—Permanence of
Paper for Printed Library Materials, ANSI/NISO Z39.48-1992.

Printed in the United States of America

For Andrea, Don, Paula, and Americans like them everywhere, who stand up every day for the natural inheritance we share and the future we create for our children.

CONTENTS

FOREWORD

BY ROBERT REDFORD

In 1903, President Theodore Roosevelt designated a tiny islet near the mouth of Florida's Indian River as the nation's first federal wildlife preserve. Over the next six years, he created dozens more, from the Gulf of Mexico to the Alaskan Yukon, carving out the toe holds in what would become the greatest national sanctuary of protected lands and wildlife anywhere in the world.

On Roosevelt's watch and in the century since then, Americans have set aside more than 635 million acres of national parks, forests, refuges, and other special places for posterity. This grand, national achievement didn't come about simply by the stroke of a pen or through the work of a single party. It was put in place over time by leaders of vision from both political camps. Each did their part to forge the broad bipartisan majority that has protected American waters and air and preserved our wildlife and lands.

Through national struggle, conflict, triumph, and war, that partnership has endured. It's a resilient part of what we believe we owe to those who have entrusted this rich inheritance to us. It is part of the promise we must keep to our children. We know this is not our inheritance alone, but a legacy of trust that is ours to honor, one American generation to the next.

"Conservation is a great moral issue," Roosevelt said, "for it involves the patriotic duty of insuring the safety and continuance of the nation."

Throughout the twentieth century, the sentiment behind those words has echoed down our government halls, on Capitol Hill, and in the White House, part of the larger commitment to our common future that leaders from both parties shared. Without that bipartisan commitment, no single party could have begun to create what together we've built—the foundation of environmental and preservation law that makes our nation stronger and enriches us all.

Today, however, that essential partnership that has served the country so well has been placed in jeopardy, as some from Roosevelt's own party seek to turn the protection of our environment into a bitterly partisan issue. Standing up for nature? That's not some party-line dispute that divides us as voters; it's a national priority that unites us as Americans.

And yet, since regaining control of the House of Representatives in 2010, the Republican majority has gone off on a tangent. In a radical departure from the party's own past and many of the central tenets of conservative thought, House Republicans have waged the single greatest legislative assault ever against the bedrock protections behind the historic gains both parties have worked so hard to achieve.

In 2011 alone, the House voted nearly 200 times to undermine existing environmental protections or delay, water down, or block outright the new standards, rules, and guidelines we need to confront emerging threats. The measures passed in the House on lopsided party-line votes, with Republicans lining up to support anti-environment proposals and Democrats arrayed on the other side.

Republicans and Democrats have long differed over how best to protect our environment while ensuring prosperity and progress for working Americans in our cities and hamlets, our factories, and farms. Never before, though, has a single party sought to unravel our environmental safety net and denigrate sound science and the policies it drives in quite the way we're seeing now. This is a threat to our future. It's putting our country at risk. And it's a problem, I believe, for American democracy.

Americans don't want our environmental protections to be eviscerated. We didn't ask our House leaders for this reckless assault. It doesn't reflect the will of the people. It echoes, instead, the same kinds of extremist voices and smokestack polluters that Teddy Roosevelt and leaders like him have been standing up to for more than a century. As Americans, we have a special responsibility, I believe, to respect and reclaim our country's rich preservationist legacy, our bipartisan record of environmental stewardship, and our shared commitment to future generations.

As parents, we teach our children to remember where we come from, to honor and treasure our roots. I believe the same great lesson applies to our political families. When we remember where we came from, Republicans and Democrats alike, we will find our way back to our environmentalist roots. We will reopen the door to the progressive solutions we need to address the challenges and embrace the opportunities of a changing world. We'll keep faith with our political forebears. And we'll keep the promise we've made to our children.

No single party can do this alone. That's the overarching lesson of the history we share. That's the central message of this book.

"Safeguarding our future is bipartisan work," Deans writes in his introduction. We must work, all of us, to help restore the bipartisan majority for our environment and to mend that torn yet still vital place in the soul of American politics. That is how we've made progress together, Republicans and Democrats, for more than a century now. And that is how we'll move forward, once more, in the challenging yet promising decades to come.

Robert Redford, the actor and director, is a trustee of the Natural Resources Defense Council.

PREFACE

BY SHERWOOD BOEHLERT

Since its dawning more than four decades ago, the modern environmental movement has been a broadly bipartisan enterprise. Republicans and Democrats have debated and discussed how best to protect our waters, wildlife, lands, and air. To be sure, we haven't always agreed. But we've worked together to get the job done, putting in place the foundational laws we all depend on to safeguard our environment and health.

And why shouldn't we? Those protections are supported by a solid majority of the American people, regardless of their political leanings. For most of us, environmental stewardship isn't a political issue; it's a part of what it means to be a responsible citizen.

Over the past year, though, we've seen a disturbing trend. Those bedrock protections we all rely upon have come under a withering partisan assault, as some have sought to turn environmental protections into an issue to divide us, red and blue.

We've seen commonsense air pollution and water quality rules attacked. We've seen funding for enforcement slashed. We've seen the authority of the Environmental Protection Agency undermined. And, perhaps most troubling of all, we've heard heated and sometimes rancorous criticism leveled at the professionals who work hard to protect our environment and hold polluters to account.

This is the wrong direction for our politics. It's the wrong direction for our country. We need to change course. We need to restore the bipartisan spirit that has enabled us to accomplish so much. We need to rebuild the environmental majority that has served us so well for so long.

This book lays the groundwork for that vital mission and makes clear why we must succeed. The stakes are too high for anything less.

Accomplishing this won't be easy. No one expects it to be. A hardening of our political culture has made the essential work of compromise difficult. Legislative options are constrained by the need to bring federal deficit spending under control. And newsroom layoffs have diminished our traditional news outlets, which are being largely supplanted by ideologically driven media that sometimes seem more interested in fanning our fears and generating anger than in conveying the larger truth about the real obstacles and opportunities we face.

Those are real problems that won't just disappear. Our country, though, has seen challenge before. Throughout our history, we've risen to it, just as we must rise today.

That doesn't mean abandoning political principles, for Democrats or Republicans. It does mean, however, that sometimes we must set aside real differences for another day, so we can find common cause in the larger good. It means that we must listen to each other more, and criticize each other less, because we never know who might come up with the solution we need. Most of all, it means working together, in good faith and good will, Republicans and Democrats alike.

Working together, we've made enormous progress cleaning up pollution and protecting our environment. We've still got a long way to go. The American consensus supporting that progress has never been stronger. We must gather that consensus, strengthen its voice, and restore the environmental majority that most faithfully reflects the will and the strength of this country.

Sherwood Boehlert is a career Republican who represented central New York State in the U.S. Congress for twenty-four years until his retirement in 2006. He served as Chairman of the House Science Committee and was a long-time member of the House Permanent Select Committee on Intelligence. He is a director of the NRDC Action Fund and a senior fellow at the Bipartisan Policy Center in Washington.

ACKNOWLEDGMENTS

I would like to thank my colleagues at the Natural Resources Defense Council and the NRDC Action Fund, the most effective environmental advocacy organizations anywhere and the Earth's best defense.

—Bob Deans

INTRODUCTION

Americans tend to think of our environment most when some kind of disaster strikes. Natural calamities, like storms or floods. Oil spills, hazardous waste leaks, and other industrial catastrophes. Beginning in early 2011, however, our environment came under a powerful and sustained assault, not by Mother Nature or some corporate misdeed, but by many of the people we elected to represent us in Washington. It is time we took note of this unfolding disaster. It is time we turned it around.

During 2011, the U.S. House of Representatives voted nearly two hundred separate times to block, delay, or weaken the commonsense safeguards we all depend on to protect our waters, wildlife, lands, and air. It was the single worst legislative assault in history on the foundational protections set in place over the past four decades by an overwhelming majority composed of Republicans and Democrats alike. This is not about jobs, as proponents claim. It's about putting polluter profits first—and putting the rest of us at risk. It's reckless. It's radical. It's relentless. It's wrong.

The campaign began with one of the first pieces of legislation the House took up in 2011—an overarching spending bill, H.R.1. It called for cutting funds for environmental protections. It would have sidelined work we must do to address emerging threats. And it was loaded down with amendments to further thwart efforts ranging from defending Appalachian forests and mountains to cleaning up the Chesapeake Bay. All that prevented that dark vision of our future from becoming law was a Senate that wouldn't go along with the anti-environment agenda in the House and a U.S. president who was equally oppposed to it.

The campaign persisted, though, through the final bill of the year, when House leaders tacked a demand for approval of a dangerous and destructive tar sands pipeline onto legislation needed to extend a payroll tax cut and unemployment benefits. And the assault continued into the opening months of 2012, when House Republicans attacked White House proposals to support the energy efficiency and renewable power development our country needs to remain successful and secure in the twenty-first century.

In each case, House leaders claim to be standing up for jobs. They are not. Jobs are lost due to business conditions, as decades of authoritative data show, and it's the economic outlook, not environmental safeguards, that drive hiring decisions on Main Street. It wasn't effective public oversight, but, rather, a lack of it, that triggered the biggest job killer of our time: the 2008 financial collapse that caused the Great Recession. And cleaning up pollution and making our homes, cars, and workplaces more efficient creates jobs—and paychecks—for millions of our workers.

Most Americans understand all this. Eight in ten want our environmental laws to be strengthened or left alone, the Pew Research Center found in a February 2012 poll. The American people don't want Congress to eviscerate our environmental protections. But someone else does—the corporate polluters that thrive by avoiding the costs of the pollution they create. All that does is impose those costs on others: the mother looking after an asthmatic child; the senior struggling with heart disease; the waterman watching fish die in polluted streams and bays; the coal miner's daughter who buries her kin while mountains are leveled and communities destroyed.

The ongoing political offensive takes aim at the protections those Americans and millions like them both need and deserve. And it serves no higher purpose than to advance the profits of companies—producers of oil, gas, and coal; operators of industrial incinerators, power plants, cement factories, and others—that together spend hundreds of millions of dollars each year to lobby Washington politicians and feed the campaign war chests of those who promote their smokestack agenda on Capitol Hill.

It's time we demanded better—for the sake of our children, for the sake of our country, and for the sake of Americans everywhere. Whatever people voted for when we elected a majority of Republicans to the House in 2010, it was almost certainly not for dirtier air and water.

In their reckless assault on the protections we all depend upon to safeguard our environment and health, the House majority turned its back on more than a century of the GOP's own history, a Republican legacy of conservation and preservation that stretches back to Theodore Roosevelt and even Abraham Lincoln. The votes betrayed the promise of environmental stewardship Republican presidents like Dwight Eisenhower, Richard Nixon, and George H. W. Bush have made to successive generations of Americans. And they cut against the grain of some of the most fundamental tenets of conservative thought, the political and philosophical cornerstones, many Republicans assert, upon which the party stands.

"What is a conservative, after all, but one who conserves," Republican President Ronald Reagan asked in 1984. "And we want to protect and conserve the land on which we live—our countryside, our rivers and mountains, our plains and meadows and forests. This is our patrimony. This is what we leave to our children. And our great moral responsibility is to leave it to them either as we found it or better than we found it."

Even from the podium of the Great Communicator himself, political leadership doesn't get much clearer than that. What a distance Reagan's party traveled to arrive at the anti-environment rampage the House majority unleashed in 2011.

"Practical conservatism degenerated into mere laudation of 'private enterprise,' economic policy almost wholly surrendered to special interests."

That's how the revered conservative writer Russell Kirk summed up the corporate hijacking of conservative ideals in the years following World War I in his 1953 treatise, *The Conservative Mind*. Did Kirk have a gift for seeing the future, or is history repeating itself? Either way, he warned, "such a nation was inviting the catastrophes which compel society to reexamine first principles."

Neither political party can empower this country to avert environmental catastrophe alone. Safeguarding our future is bipartisan work, as leaders from both parties have long understood. Exactly how we go about that has always been the subject of honest and reasoned debate, reflecting genuine philosophical differences between Republicans and Democrats. In 2011, though, and the early months of 2012, something very different was at play in the House.

With more than fourteen million Americans unemployed, and much of the country angry and looking for someone to blame, Republicans regained control of the House in the 2010 midterm elections, largely on the strength of the national tea party movement. That movement coalesced around grassroots activists, right-wing media impresarios, and scores of millions of dollars from old-line corporate polluters looking to wed their anti-regulatory agenda to the frustrations of millions of ordinary Americans who mostly just wanted to get back to work.

And the House leadership told them a whopper: if we could just do away with those pesky environmental regulations, and cut taxes a little bit more, we'll free corporations everywhere to invest rising profits to hire more workers.

If that were true, we wouldn't be in the worst jobs market in thirty years; we'd be in the greatest hiring boom in history. That's because corporate profits hit $2 trillion in 2011, an all-time high, both in dollars and as a percentage of gross domestic product. Corporate profits, in fact, were a staggering $566 billion above the historical average, as a percentage of GDP.

That profit premium could create a lot of jobs if what House Republicans told us were true. Economists know, and the rest of us learned, that's simply not how it works.

Businesses hire people to create or respond to demand. That's pretty much it. And when consumers start buying again, as is slowly happening, more Americans will go back to work. No one should be fooled, though, into believing we can change the immutable laws of supply and demand by stripping ourselves of the foundational environmental safeguards created over the past forty years by Republicans and Democrats alike, leaders of vision and courage who stood up together for nature and put into place the responsible public oversight we all depend on to protect our environment and health.

It's time we stood up for that once again.

Washington, March, 2012

1

WASTELAND

Imagine some of the last wild streams in Appalachia buried forever beneath toxic rubble dumped by coal companies that blast ancient mountains to pieces and lay ruin to thousands of acres of land. Picture children born with so much mercury in their formative brains that they come into the world with a strike against them, their mental development impeded, and their ability to learn impaired by the powerful neurotoxin poured into our air from industrial smokestacks. Envision our nation's largest and most important estuary, the Chesapeake Bay, as a barren tidal wasteland, a reeking dead zone of aquatic decay, where dwindling numbers of fish, crabs, and birds struggle to survive; a vacant, brackish, dismal void where algae-blooms choke the life from waters and swimming and fishing are things of the past.

No elected leader would openly advocate that nightmare vision of our environment and health. And yet, it's a fair take on the future that the U.S. House of Representatives voted to create during 2011, part of the single worst legislative assault ever waged against the foundational safeguards that protect our air, water, wildlife, and lands.

With overwhelming support from its Republican majority, and a handful of Democrats, the House voted in February to allow Appalachian waterways to be ravaged by coal companies. It voted in September to defer, indefinitely, rules to reduce the mercury, soot, and other air pollution that factories and power plants spew into our air. And it voted in February to block long overdue plans to save the Chesapeake Bay from being polluted, quite literally, to death.

Those votes, moreover, were just a few salvos in a much wider campaign.

Over the course of 2011, House Republican leaders ordered more than 190 votes on measures that would have weakened environmental safeguards, prevented rules from being enforced, or derailed the introduction of pro-environment policies. The assault began with one of the first pieces of legislation the House took up—an overarching spending bill, H.R. 1—and continued to the body's final action of the year—tacking a demand for White House approval of the Keystone XL tar sands pipeline to must-pass legislation extending payroll tax cuts and unemployment benefits. The tally of votes—in committees and by the full House—was compiled by staffers of the House Energy and Commerce Committee and posted on the panel's minority web site, an extraordinary step meant to document the actions of what the site calls "the most anti-environment House in history."

In a year marked by bitter partisanship, the question of environmental protections split the House like no other issue. In lopsided votes one after another, ayes and nays were cast mostly along party lines. All but a handful of the body's 242 Republicans banded together to undermine policies that protect our environment and health, while the vast majority of its 192 Democrats voted the other way. On a few measures, Republicans were joined by a dozen or so Democrats, generally from states heavily dependent on fossil fuel production or use.

The votes targeted the effectiveness of bedrock legislation like the Clean Air Act, the Clean Water Act, and the Endangered Species Act. They went after forward-leaning clean energy policies. And they attacked essential oversight watchdogs like the Environmental Protection Agency. The votes took aim at laws, measures, and institutions put in place with the support of Republicans and Democrats alike, at a time when standing up for nature was a national priority that enjoyed broad bipartisan support. In 2011, though, House Republicans rejected that proud bipartisan past and instead voted for bills favored by oil and gas companies, coal producers, refinery, incinerator and power plant owners, cement factory operators, and other top line polluters. In doing so, they struck at commonsense public oversight and put our environment and health at risk, from the air we breathe to the water we drink, from the mountains to the sea.

"This is the most anti-environmental House of Representatives in history," said the House Energy and Commerce committee's ranking

Democrat, Henry Waxman of California, who has served in the House for nearly forty years. "So far this Congress, the House of Representatives, has voted again and again to block action to address climate change, to halt efforts to reduce air and water pollution, to undermine protections for public lands and coastal areas and to weaken the protection of the environment in other ways," Waxman said during a Capitol Hill hearing September 22, 2011.

CONSERVATION IS CONSERVATIVE

It isn't only Democrats who are alarmed at the GOP's concerted assault and the vision of environmental backsliding behind it.

"I've been appalled," said former New Jersey Gov. Christine Todd Whitman, a Republican who served as administrator of the Environmental Protection Agency under President George W. Bush. "The vision, I think, is to just do away with the EPA, and I think that is a disaster," she said. "The American people don't want that."

"I am very disappointed," echoed another career Republican, William Reilly, who led the EPA under Bush's father, President George H. W. Bush. In a November 2011 speech, Reilly lambasted members of his party for what he called "demagogic assaults on regulators who are doing the job Congress gave them," in implementing the Clean Air Act amendments that the senior Bush signed.

In separate telephone interviews, both Reilly and Whitman said the long train of anti-environmental votes by House Republicans represents a sharp and abrupt departure for a party that traces its environmental roots to the presidency of Abraham Lincoln, the Republican who first began protecting public lands from commercial development.

"Conservation is a great moral issue, for it involves the patriotic duty of insuring the safety and continuance of the nation," Theodore Roosevelt, the first Republican president of the twentieth century, said in 1910. By then, building on what Lincoln began, Roosevelt had created more than fifty federal wildlife reserves and parks, establishing the preservation of our natural heritage as an American priority that has since led us to set aside, as a nation, more than 635 million acres of national parks, forests, refuge areas, waterways, and federally managed lands for posterity.

"Republicans have been part of the environmental movement since the get go," Whitman said, "and it just drives me nuts that we now seem to be walking away from it as if were something bad or we don't believe in science or the environment, because, to me, conservation is conservative, and that ought to be part of what we're about."

A TOXIC BREW

In 2011, though, the Republican Party fell under the sway of the new "tea party" faction, which hews well to the right of the GOP mainstream and is more than twice as hostile toward environmental safeguards, polls show, as traditional Republicans. The tea party movement, moreover, is heavily financed by deep-pocketed industrial polluters, which have long sought to eviscerate environmental protections for the sake of increased profits. Backed by conservative news media and talk show hosts, the tea party and its corporate benefactors pushed House Republicans far off the path of environmental stewardship their party forebears had blazed.

Many Republicans are uneasy with the dramatic shift. Some appear to have succumbed to tea party pressure, or fear of being defeated by tea party challengers, to support anti-environmental measures they figured were unlikely to become law. Indeed, few of the House measures have made it through the Senate, where a razor-thin Democratic majority has either rejected the House environmental bills or not yet acted on them.

"You have a lot of moderate Republicans who generally would not support this legislation, but they saw what happened in 2010, with the rise of the tea party candidates," explained Jim DiPeso, spokesman for Republicans for Environmental Protection, a nonprofit Washington advocacy group. In an effort to appeal to that right-wing base, and draw political distinctions between the GOP and the agenda of President Obama, "The political calculus was made to develop a narrative that government regulation is at the heart of our economic problems," DiPeso said. That's not the case, he said, but "that's the origin of this wave of legislation that you're seeing."

Votes, though, count for something more than simply scoring political points or appeasing the party's more extreme constituents. Votes are how elected leaders publicly signal their priorities and beliefs. And they are the way our democracy provides the rest of us the chance to hold representatives accountable to the people they serve. With a different makeup in the Senate, after all, or a different president in the White House, much of the House GOP vision might come to pass.

Senate Democrats, of late, haven't exactly distinguished themselves as environmental champions. In 2009, a Democrat-led Senate allowed comprehensive energy and climate legislation to die due to filibuster by failing to take up a good bill the House had approved. The next year, the Democratic majority in the Senate allowed the same fate to befall a bill the House passed that would have strengthened safeguards for offshore drilling in the wake of the BP blowout in the Gulf of Mexico. Those were tremendous failures at a time when Democrats held a majority of the seats in both houses of Congress.

The midterm elections of 2010, however, gave the Republicans control of the House. Going after needed environmental safeguards is how the party's leaders chose to devote much of their effort and time. That, too, has real consequences for the nation.

Amid the rancor of tax and budget questions, and social dilemmas that both parties have used to drive a political wedge to split their opponents, protecting our environment and health should be goals that rally all sides. After all, there's a strong national consensus in support of those objectives.

Half the nation wants our environmental protections to be strengthened, while another 29 percent want them to be left as they are, the Pew Research Center found in a February 2012 poll of 1,501 adults nationwide. Only 17 percent said those safeguards should be weakened, despite the GOP's year-long effort to denigrate needed protections and those who enforce them. Even among Republican voters, a solid majority—58 percent—favors strengthening environmental protections or leaving them alone, the poll found.

"Environmental and health threats are unambiguous, nonpartisan concerns. They affect us whether we live in a red state or a blue state," EPA Administrator Lisa Jackson said in a November 2011 speech at the University of Wisconsin. "Contrary to more divisive issues, people of all backgrounds want swift action when they see these threats in their communities."

For decades, that common support for clean water and air, healthy wildlife and lands, has animated the political exchange in Washington.

Politicians debated the scope and reach of environmental protections, to be sure, along lines reflecting robust yet reasoned philosophical differences between Republicans and Democrats and even, for that matter, within the parties themselves. In 2011, though, something very different was at play in the House. Congressional observers who recall the strong majorities from both parties that joined to pass landmark environmental protections four decades ago were shocked by the partisan rancor that split and largely paralyzed the Congress in 2011, plunging its public approval ratings to historic lows.

"It's been discouraging," said DiPeso. "A lot of these laws were passed at a time when Republicans and Democrats worked together with some degree of comity to reach a compromise," he said. "That's the kind of dynamic we'd like to see again. Right now, we don't see that."

A CAUSE BEYOND PARTY AND BEYOND FACTIONS

It was Republican President Richard Nixon, after all, who created the Environmental Protection Agency in 1970 and signed into law the foundational National Environmental Policy Act of 1969. That act established the White House Council on Environmental Quality and laid the cornerstone for a new body of federal law based on the need to protect the environment and public health from pollution. That was a signal year for our environment. An offshore blowout gushed four million gallons of crude oil into the waters off the coast of Santa Barbara, California. Industrial chemicals coursed so freely through the nation's heartland that Ohio's Cuyahoga River caught fire. And Los Angeles became the world capital of smog. Against that background of degradation and the urgency it conferred, the groundbreaking National Environmental Policy Act passed unanimously in the Senate and by a 372–15 margin in the House.

"Restoring nature to its natural state is a cause beyond party and beyond factions," Nixon told the country in his 1970 State of the Union address. "It has become a common cause of all the people of this country," he said, calling on Congress to strengthen environmental safeguards, invest in cleaner fuels, promote more efficient cars, and crack down on corporate polluters. "Clean air, clean water, open spaces, these should once again be the birthright of every American," said Nixon. "If we act now, they can be."

On Nixon's watch, Congress also passed the Clean Air Act, the Endangered Species Act, the Clean Water Act, and other fundamental protections. Each was criticized, in its time, by big polluters who claimed the safeguards would cripple our national economy. Instead, we had economic growth averaging 3.2 percent per year during the following decade 1971–1980.

In 1970, the country kicked out $1 trillion worth of goods and services. By 1980, that figure had grown to $2.8 trillion. Since then, our economy has continued to grow, as we've cut the pollution that causes acid rain, lead poisoning, smog, and other threats by 60 percent, saving hundreds of millions of lives and trillions of dollars in health care and clean-up costs, while making life better for Americans everywhere.

"The destiny of our land, the air we breathe, the water we drink, is not in the mystical hands of an uncontrollable agent," Nixon said in a radio address from the Oval Office on Valentine's Day 1973, calling on the nation once again to summon the political will to stand up to big polluters for the sake of generations to come. "A future which brings the balancing of our resources—preserving quality with quantity—is a future limited only by the boundaries of our will to get the job done."

For House Republicans, those boundaries were starkly drawn in 2011. Influenced by its tea party wing, corporate lobbyists, and cash donations from powerful industries, Republicans in the House adopted a reckless and radical vision that put polluters first, turning their backs on their party's own history and many conventions of traditional conservative thought. They did so repeatedly under the guise of job creation, a political play on a beleaguered public struggling with the highest unemployment levels since Ronald Reagan was president.

"The people of America understand that the EPA is, in fact, killing jobs," Rep. Morgan Griffith, R-VA, said in October 2011, while advocating for legislation that blocked a new EPA rule to cut air pollution from incinerators and industrial boilers. Griffith is part of the freshman class of Republicans elected to Congress in 2010 by voters stoked on anti-government rage. His campaign received extensive backing from Americans for Prosperity, a political action committee, or PAC, that advocates cuts in taxes and government regulations. It was founded by

David Koch. His family's privately held Koch Industries—an oil refining, pipeline, paper, and chemicals conglomerate based in Wichita, Kansas—is the tenth largest polluter in the nation, the University of Massachusetts' Political Economy Research Institute found using EPA emissions data. In railing out against the EPA, which regulates much of the Koch empire, Griffith cited the need to protect jobs and owners of large boilers in his southwest Virginia district, asserting that their concerns were poorly understood by regulators "here in the ivory towers of Washington."

In fact, the most authoritative economic data available—from the U.S. Labor Department's Bureau of Labor Statistics—shows that federal regulations, of all kinds, account for less than 1 percent of American job loss. The truth is, environmental safeguards protect and even create jobs, promote economic growth, and more than pay for themselves through the manifest benefits they provide.

"For decades, corporations and their trade associations have opposed regulations aimed at protecting human health and the environment," states a 2010 report by the conservation arm of the Pew Charitable Trusts, a nonprofit public interest organization. "Industry has repeatedly argued that the cost of complying is too high, the benefits to society don't justify the investment, or the regulations will cost jobs," the report continued, citing corporate opposition to everything from getting lead and asbestos out of our homes to putting seat belts and air bags in our cars. "In fact, regulatory requirements to protect the environment, workers and consumers have often led to innovation, increased productivity and new businesses and jobs."

In 1970, for example, Nixon signed the Clean Air Act. It was strengthened by amendments in 1990 that were signed by another Republican, President George H. W. Bush, after those amendments passed in the House by a margin of 401–21 and in the Senate 89–11. In 2010, the EPA calculates, the provisions of this act prevented 160,000 premature deaths, 130,000 heart attacks, and 1.7 million cases of aggravated asthma. That enabled Americans to avoid more than 16 million lost days at work or school. Those benefits were worth an estimated $1.3 trillion that year, the agency estimated, compared with costs of $53 billion that year to comply with the law. Every dollar invested in clean air, in other words, generated, on average, $25 worth of benefits.

"Say what you want about EPA's business sense, but we know how to get a return on an investment," EPA Administrator Jackson said in a 2010 agency speech marking the fortieth anniversary of the Clean Air Act. "The Clean Air Act is one of the most cost-effective things the American people have done for themselves in the last half century. The irony is that one of the most economically successful programs in American history is also one of the most economically maligned."

And that was before the 2011 legislative broadside, when House Republicans voted seventy-seven times to reject measures that would improve air quality or to block, delay, or undermine long overdue air pollution rules—such as new standards to reduce the chemicals and soot belched into our air by industrial incinerators, factories, and power plants.

Largely along party-line votes, the House also sought to:

—prohibit the EPA and the Army Corps of Engineers from protecting small streams, wetlands, and tributaries under the Clean Water Act.
—cut funding for advanced energy research, renewable power development, and efficiency gains.
—transfer valuable public lands to mining companies, skipping over environmental review required by law.

With similarly partisan votes, the House blocked measures that would:

—protect the Great Lakes from mercury and other toxic air pollution.
—support studies needed to defend endangered species.
—moderate off-road vehicle use in our national forests.

IT'S NOT ABOUT SCIENCE, IT'S ABOUT POLITICS

In a sweeping action that laid bare the bitterly partisan environmental divide, the House voted in April to prohibit the EPA from writing new rules to reduce factory and power plant emissions of industrial carbon emissions, methane, and other greenhouse gases that are warming the planet. The EPA is authorized to regulate such pollution through the Clean Air Act, authorization that was confirmed in a 5–4 Supreme Court ruling in 2007. The House vote was 255–172 in favor of repealing EPA's authority to help combat climate change; 236 Republicans voted for the repeal and 172 Democrats voted against it. Not a single Republican voted to oppose the measure; 19 Democrats voted for it.

The measure was authored by House Energy and Commerce Committee Chairman Fred Upton, R-MI. Two of the nation's largest emitters of the carbon pollution that's accelerating climate change—the electric utility and oil and gas industries—together contributed $290,700 to Upton's 2010 reelection campaign. Since he was first elected to Congress in 1987, Upton has received $958,778 in campaign contributions from the two industries, according to the Center for Responsive Politics, a nonpartisan research outfit that tracks influence peddling in Washington.

On an even stricter party-line vote, the House rejected, 240–184, an amendment simply stating that Congress accepts the EPA's findings that climate change is real, puts public health at risk, and is caused largely by human activities. Only 1 Republican—Rep. Dave Reichert, R-WA— agreed with the statement: 237 of his GOP colleagues rejected it.

Unfortunately, we can't simply vote down climate change, no matter how much we wish we could. The planet is warming in ways that threaten us all. A roomful of politicians declared that it isn't. That changes nothing except our ability to do something to address the gathering threat. Here are the facts.

The year House Republicans rejected climate change was the eleventh hottest year on record. It was the thirty-fifth year in a row that the annual global temperature was above the twentieth-century average. The eleven years since 2001 all rank among the thirteen hottest years since 1880. How do we know? These are the findings of the National Oceanic and Atmospheric Administration, the single most authoritative source for global climate data in the world.

The rise in global temperature—2011 was 0.92 degrees Fahrenheit above the twentieth-century average of 57 degrees—is having dramatic impacts around the world. It's melting the Arctic ice cap, to cite a single overarching example. Over the past thirty years, we've lost roughly one third of the Arctic Ocean ice cap. We've lost enough ice, due to climate change, to cover the entire eastern third of the United States, from the Mississippi River to the Atlantic Ocean. How do we know that? Because the United States Air Force flies a satellite over the ice cap every 102 minutes. The satellite sends back images of the ice fourteen times a day. That's not a tree-hugger operation: it's part of the Pentagon's Defense Meteorological Satellite Program, which helps enable the military to plan its global operations without having to listen to the Weather Channel. The imagery is analyzed by the National Snow & Ice Data Center operated by the National Aeronautics and Space Administration—the people who put a man on the moon. They know what's happening to the Arctic ice because they have thirty years of pictures that tell them. The ice is melting, and it's not coming back. We've been losing it at the rate of about 12 percent each decade, since 1979. Within another few decades, we could see summers where the Arctic sea ice is gone.

The planet is warming. That is not in doubt. Natural causes play a role. That role has been overwhelmed, however, by the carbon pollution and other greenhouse gases we are pumping into the atmosphere through the production and consumption of coal, oil, and natural gas. How do we know that? Because the best climate scientists in the world, people who make their living studying this and know what they're talking about, say so.

"Climate change is occurring, is very likely caused primarily by the emission of greenhouse gases from human activities, and poses significant risks for a range of human and natural systems. Emissions continue to increase, which will result in further change and greater risks. Responding to those risks is a crucial challenge facing the United States and the world today and for many decades to come."

That comes from the National Academies of Science 2011 report entitled *America's Climate Choices*. The National Academies of Science was chartered by the U.S. Congress in 1863 and directed to "investigate, examine, experiment, and report on any subject of science or art," at the request of the U.S. government. It is our national scientific brain trust, the place we go when we need to understand the bedrock truth about our world, as best as can possibly be known. The climate report is the product of hundreds of peer-reviewed analyses and exhaustive studies by scientists who sign their names to their work and stake their professional reputations on their findings. The report was put together under the supervision of twenty-two senior scholars in their field from institutions such as Duke University, Michigan State, Georgia Tech, Stanford, Princeton, and the Massachusetts Institute of Technology.

At some point, the reasonable person has to ask: what exactly do the House Republicans know that these guys haven't figured out?

"Scientifically, there is no controversy. Politically, there is a controversy, because there are political interest groups making it a controversy," Harry Lambright, a Syracuse University professor of public policy who specializes in environment, science and technology issues, told the Associated Press in February 2012. "It's not about science. It's about politics."

We all have a right to our opinion. Something is badly askew, however, when the weight and consensus of the scientific world can be callously tossed aside by politicians who refuse to face facts and instead insist on blocking every reasonable attempt to begin the vital process of reducing the industrial carbon pollution that is changing our climate and threatening us all. That sorry spectacle was on vivid display in the 2011 House of Representatives.

Some votes have targeted the very process of responsible public oversight that has served the nation well for decades. In putting in place policies to defend our environment and health, our government has long relied on the rule of law and the reason of science in a transparent and open process subject to extensive public comment and exhaustive court review. House Republicans this year voted, instead, to toss out that proven combination in favor of a political jump ball. In December, on a party-line vote of 241–184, the House majority passed legislation—given the sprightly moniker "Regulations from the Executive in Need of Scrutiny Act"—that would enable either house of Congress to kill any significant regulation, either by voting it down or simply not passing it within seventy days. Seventy days? This is the Congress, remember, that drove the country to the brink of default in August 2011 because it was still struggling after months of partisan wrangling to raise the debt ceiling to cover the spending it had already agreed to. Setting congressional dysfunction aside, the so-called REINS Act would turn the vital tasks of public oversight into a political sweepstakes that empowers corporate polluters and others with the richest or loudest voice to determine the outcome of any contest that pits their profits against the public good. Do smokestack lobbyists and the industrial chieftains they represent really need the help?

SOME EVIL GENIE AT THE EPA

The GOP's legislative offensive was augmented by a yearlong attack against the EPA, waged from Capitol Hill to the presidential caucus rooms of Iowa. In Congress and on the campaign trail, Republicans blamed the EPA for the high unemployment rates and economic downturn that were triggered by the Wall Street collapse of 2008.

"Many of us think that the overregulation from EPA is at the heart of our stalled economy," Rep. Mike Simpson, R-ID, told *The New York Times* in an article published July 27, 2011, under the headline "Republicans Seek Big Cuts in Environmental Rules."

Rep. Joe Barton, R-TX, used language Republican presidents had reserved for Cold War rivals and terrorist states in asserting that something "evil" was afoot at the EPA.

"It's as if there is some evil genie at the EPA that is bound and determined to put every regulation possible on the books as soon as possible, regardless of the economic consequences," Barton scolded EPA Administrator Jackson during a September 2011 hearing on Capitol Hill.

Barton is the House member, by the way, who publicly apologized to BP's Chief Executive Officer Tony Hayward after President Obama secured a $20 billion escrow fund from the British oil company to cover damages from the 2010 Deepwater Horizon blowout in the Gulf of Mexico. Barton referred to the fund as a White House "shakedown." He has received $1.6 million in campaign contributions from the oil and gas industry since 1989—more than any other member of the House— according to the Center for Responsive Politics. His campaigns have received another $1.4 million from the electric utilities industry, the largest coal burners in the country.

"Is it the goal of the EPA to get to zero emissions," Barton badgered Jackson, "i.e., basically shut down the U.S. economy?"

No, Jackson could only reply, "Of course not, sir."

Shutting down the EPA was the goal, though, for GOP presidential hopeful Rep. Michelle Bachmann, R-MN, who spent much of the year calling for the dismantling of the EPA. "It should really be renamed the job-killing organization of America," Bachmann said in a GOP debate in June 2011. Her fellow House Republicans voted in February 2011 to slash agency funding by a third, cuts meant to cripple the EPA and its ability to produce and enforce needed safeguards.

At times, the Republican offensive ran counter to longstanding tenets of conservative thought, like the values of thrift, efficiency, and self-reliance. With 2.7 million Americans already working to develop wind, solar, and other renewable sources of domestic power, or to build the next generation of energy-efficient cars, homes, and workplaces, some Republicans disparaged the effort or sought to politicize it, the first step toward turning a national goal into a partisan football.

"The guise of 'green jobs' has become a political rallying cry aimed to unite environmentalists and union leaders in a deliberate effort to consolidate an ideologically based agenda," reads a September 2011 report by the Republican staff of the House Committee on Oversight and Government Reform. The report was part of a broader effort that sought to demonize President Obama for proposing policies aimed at helping American workers succeed in a global clean energy market worth more than $260 billion a year. "How Obama's Green Energy Agenda is Killing Jobs," was the title the committee's chairman, Darrell Issa, R-CA, gave to a September hearing. Issa accused Obama of waging a "propaganda" campaign to tout green jobs. Those jobs, meanwhile, were providing nearly three million American families an economic lifeline in tough times. That's not propaganda, it's progress, but that didn't stop the Republican attacks that, at times, descended into ridicule on the floor of the House.

"The mere phrase 'the regulators' brings fear and trepidation down into the hearts and souls of small business owners throughout the fruited plain," Rep. Ted Poe, R-TX, said during a December debate centered on the regulatory process. "They sit around a big oak table, drinking their lattes, they have out their iPads and their computers, and they decide: 'Who shall we regulate today?'"

I WILL SHOW YOU FEAR
IN A HANDFUL OF DUST

This kind of reckless, sustained, and comprehensive assault on commonsense safeguards, clean energy advances that can reduce our reliance on foreign oil, and the agency that defends our environment and health would, at any time, put the country at risk. It is particularly perilous now for three reasons.

First, we're entering a historic domestic energy boom. Expansive new oil and gas discoveries are driving drilling and production to levels not seen in decades. With that activity, though, come new technologies, operations, and risks. Decades of damage, irreversible and widespread, lie ahead if we now turn our back on the kinds of protections we need to get this right.

Second, even as our domestic gas and oil supplies increase, we're in the opening stages of a clean energy revolution that is remaking our economy and reshaping the world. If the opportunity, though, is global, so is the competition. Countries like China, Germany, India, and others are organizing national policies and resources around the need to succeed in a worldwide green technology sector on track to top $3 trillion over the coming decade. We cannot afford to sideline American workers in this global contest for jobs and growth while other nations make sure their people have the tools they need to succeed.

Finally, the demands that global growth is placing on the natural resources of the world, and the damage so far done to our planet, have left us no choice but to turn away from the destructive ways of the past and embark on a more sustainable path. We cannot return to the days when companies clear-cut, strip-mined, and smoke-stacked themselves to prosperity while impoverishing entire peoples and destroying their lands. That is something our economy won't support and our planet won't survive. And, just as important in a democracy, it is something the American people won't tolerate, no matter which political party they back, no matter where in our country they live.

Born in St. Louis and educated at Harvard, the Sorbonne and Oxford, T. S. Eliot was a Nobel laureate, a towering poet, and social critic widely regarded as the twentieth-century's preeminent conservative man of letters. In the years following World War I, Eliot captured the sense of spiritual decline and societal despair echoing through his generation in his epic poem "The Waste Land." It contains a passage with a haunting resemblance to the environmental devastation left in the wake of modern day industrial practices, oil, gas, and coal development and the ravages of global climate change.

"A heap of broken images, where the sun beats," the lines read, "And the dead tree gives no shelter, the cricket no relief, / And the dry stone no sound of water," Eliot writes. "I will show you fear, in a handful of dust."

What stands between our world and Eliot's apocalyptic vision of waste and ruin is the foundation of environmental safeguards that were put in place over the past four decades by overwhelming majorities of Republicans and Democrats alike. In waging a reckless, sustained, and concerted assault on that foundation, House Republicans have shown us fear, not in a handful of dust, but in a torrent of bad legislation that has put our future at risk.

2

FROM THE MOUNTAINS
TO THE SEA

Coal mining, its dangers and the destruction it leaves, have been part of life for more than a century in West Virginia's sparsely populated Logan County. Forty years ago, 125 people were killed there, when heavy rains washed out the dam at a pond of mining waste. The break sent 132 million gallons of toxic coal slurry thundering down tiny Buffalo Creek, swallowing up seventeen communities in a raging wall of fury rising twenty feet above its banks.

Even in coal-dependent Logan County, though, the plans for the Spruce No. 1 mine were a jolt to the sensibilities.

To get at a seam of bituminous coal, the Mingo Logan Coal Company proposed to blast away ancient mountains 400 feet tall and otherwise lay waste to 2,278 acres of land, an area roughly the size of downtown Pittsburgh. The waste from the project, one of the largest so-called "mountaintop removal" operations ever undertaken in West Virginia, would be dumped into a series of nearby streams and tributaries, burying forever some seven miles of Appalachian waterways beneath 110 million cubic yards of rock, dirt, and toxic coal mine waste.

The streams—the Pigeonroost Branch and Oldhouse Branch—gather some of the cleanest waters in the Appalachians, one of the oldest mountain chains anywhere in the world. From there, the waters make their way through the regional watershed to the great Ohio River, the Mississippi, and all the way to the Gulf of Mexico.

The imperiled streams support a rich web of life that includes deer, raccoons, mayflies, woodpeckers, salamanders, and smallmouth bass. The project would destroy both of those streams and pollute waters and habitat for miles downstream with coal dust and other sediments laden with salt, selenium, and other toxic pollution in violation of the U.S. Clean Water Act.

The coal company's long fight for a federal permit to fill in the streams with toxic scree pitted local and national environmental concerns against the company's claim that the project would support 250 jobs. The assertion was embraced by industry backers, while opponents of mountaintop removal feared the company would strip out the coal, pocket the profits and leave ruin in its wake, an old and sorry story across much of the Mountain State.

"The coal industry will get their piece of the pie. But it doesn't make it right for companies to bury our rivers and streams, poisoning our children and destroying communities," Paula Swearengin, a West Virginia opponent of mountaintop removal, said at a 2010 public hearing on the Spruce No. 1 mine. "Clean water should not be an option in America; it's a right," said Swearengin, whose father and grandfather were coal miners. "And a miner should not have to choose between poisoning their child and his job."

The Environmental Protection Agency agreed. In January 2011, after extensive review, some 50,000 public comments and more than a year of unsuccessful EPA efforts to get the mining company to come up with an alternative plan, the EPA withdrew a 2007 permit the U.S. Army Corps of Engineers had granted to allow waste from the Spruce No. 1 mine to bury local streams.

"The proposed Spruce No. 1 mine would use destructive and unsustainable mining practices that jeopardize the health of Appalachian communities and clean water on which they depend," EPA's assistant administrator for water, Peter Silva, explained in a press statement, citing the prospect of "irreversible damage to water quality."

Immediately, the coal industry's man in Washington struck back, and his fellow House Republicans joined him.

During the first nine months of 2011, Rep. David McKinley, R-WV, received $153,378 in political contributions from individuals and organizations involved in coal mining. That's more than any other member of Congress took in from the industry that year, according to the Center for Responsive Politics.

A civil engineer by training, McKinley is serving his first term in Congress, part of the freshman class of tea party candidates swept into office on a wave of angry, anti-government sentiment. As a recipient of coal money, he's just getting started. Senate Minority Leader Mitch Mc-Connell, R-KY, is the lifetime coal cash leader on Capitol Hill, having received $494,299 in campaign contributions from the industry during the course of his career.

On February 18, weeks after the EPA stood up to protect irreplaceable Appalachian waters and habitats, McKinley rose in the well of the House to cut the legs out from under the agency. He proposed an amendment to a huge federal spending bill that would block the EPA from withdrawing the permit.

"We all should be concerned about the recent actions by the EPA and how it continues to destroy jobs by exceeding its statutory authority as envisioned by Congress," McKinley said. He went on to accuse the agency of waging a "relentless war on coal," warning darkly of the "dangerous precedent" the EPA decision had set. "If the EPA can be allowed to retroactively revoke a permit in West Virginia, they can continue this onslaught wherever water permits exist throughout America."

The Clean Water Act gives the EPA explicit authority to cancel Army Corps of Engineers permits for projects that the agency believes pose unacceptable risks to waters, fisheries, or wildlife. The EPA, however, rarely does so. In fact, while the Corps of Engineers processes about 60,000 permit requests a year, the EPA has struck down just thirteen—including the Spruce No.1 mine—in the past four decades. That's hardly an "onslaught," by any account, and it certainly constitutes no threat to water permits in general.

"Only in the most egregious instances has EPA used this authority," Rep. Jim Moran, D-VA, argued during the brief House debate over McKinley's bill. "It's understandable that mining companies don't want any restriction on their mining," said Moran, the ranking Democrat on the House Appropriations subcommittee on the Interior and Environment. "But it's not excusable for this Congress to prevent the EPA from carrying out its lawful responsibilities and not to heed the long-term health impacts on the American people and of the quality of water in these regions."

That, though, is precisely what the Republican-controlled House voted to do, after another coal industry advocate, Rep. Hal Rogers, R-KY, called the EPA's action on the Spruce No. 1 mine "the poster child for EPA's overreach." In the two decades he has represented the coal country of eastern Kentucky, Rogers, chairman of the House Appropriations Committee, has received $358,524 in campaign contributions from the mining industry, according to the Center for Responsive Politics.

At two o'clock in the morning on February 19, a bitterly divided House voted to strip the EPA of its authority to keep the Mingo Logan Coal Company from destroying Appalachian streams. The vote was 240–182. Among Republicans, 223 supported the bill, 14 voted against it, while 168 Democrats opposed the measure, and 17 supported it.

The vote ripped through the heart of West Virginia coal country like dynamite blasting open a seam. Where, many wondered, was the much-promised legislation to improve miner safety in the wake of the 2010 explosion that killed twenty-nine West Virginia workers at the Upper Big Branch mine? As of early 2012, nearly two years after the disaster, neither the House nor the Senate had gotten around to passing such a bill, a failing *The New York Times* rightly called "a national disgrace." And yet, when coal company profits were put at risk to save irreplaceable mountains and waters, the House took action to defend the industry within weeks.

"I think we have the best paid politicians that the coal industry can buy," Paula Swearengin, the mountaintop removal opponent, said in a telephone interview from her home outside of Beckley. "The people of Appalachia are treated like we're just disposable casualties of the coal industry," said Swearengin, a member of the board of directors of the Keeper of the Mountian Foundation in Charleston, West Virginia. "We live in the land of the lost, because nobody wants to hear us."

ANDREA'S CHOICE

A divorced mother of three grown children, Andrea Roberts found herself at one of life's crossroads in 2008. And so, when the offer came through for a job as a pharmacist in Cleveland, she girded herself for the move from upstate New York and the chance to make a fresh start in a new home.

What she hadn't counted on was Cleveland's air pollution, and the toll it would take on her health. The American Lung Association ranks

Cleveland as the twelfth worst city in the country when it comes to the fine particles of metals, acids, smoke, and dirt that make up soot belched into the air by area factories, cars, trucks, and coal-fired power plants. It also gets poor marks on smog and toxic air pollutants like mercury, arsenic, and selenium, both regionally produced and swept in from the vast industrial region upwind of Cleveland. Area power plants and factories pumped 65 million pounds of pollutants into the air in 2010 alone, accounting for about 7.6 percent of the national total from large factories and plants.

Breathing in Cleveland, it turned out, was bad for Andrea's health. The air there aggravated her asthma so much she could barely go outdoors throughout much of the year. She developed chronic bronchitis that kept her out of work for five weeks one winter and nearly landed her in the hospital.

"Unless I got in a car and drove for 45 minutes, I couldn't go out for a walk," Roberts explained. "I started feeling like the world was eating me up."

She's hardly alone. Among the 2.9 million people living in the greater Cleveland-Akron area, nearly 300,000 have asthma, the lung association reports. About 63,000 of those are children, whose developing lungs are especially vulnerable to the risks of breathing dirty air. Statewide, asthma kills 160 people each year, sends 63,000 to the emergency room and results in hospitalization for 18,000, according to the recent report "The Burden of Asthma in Ohio" by the state department of health.

Several things can contribute to asthma, including poor air quality in the home. Breathing air loaded down with soot and toxic chemicals, however, aggravates the condition, increases the incidents of asthma attacks and results in more frequent need for medical attention.

"Asthma's the canary in the coal mine," said Sumita Khatri, MD, a specialist in pulmonary disease and asthma at the Cleveland Clinic, one of the nation's top-ranked hospitals. "When air quality is poorer, from the standpoint of particulate matter, there seems to be an increase in the number of visits to the emergency room for asthma," she said. "Cleveland is a very good example."

For Andrea, that finally meant setting aside her dream of building a new life in the Midwest to preserve what was left of her health.

"I probably was putting my life at stake, or shortening it," she said. "It became an overwhelming feeling that I needed to do something for my health and get out of there."

And so, just before Thanksgiving of 2011, she said goodbye to the new friends she'd made, loaded up her Subaru and made the six-hour drive back to upstate New York, in search of cleaner air.

"Leaving was, in many ways, very sad, because I was making my own stand there, taking back my life, taking charge," she said. "I tried really hard not to feel like a failure."

AIR RAID

While Andrea struggled with her wrenching choice, House Republicans in Washington were hard at work on a series of measures to block, water down, or delay for years the very national actions that could help clean up the air in Cleveland and other places around the country. The year began with Republicans passing, on a party-line vote, a spending bill in February that singled out the EPA for deep budget cuts. In addition, the House tacked on several amendments to the spending bill that would, among other things:

- Prohibit the EPA from regulating factory, refinery, and power plant emissions of carbon dioxide, methane, nitrous oxide, and other pollutants known as greenhouse gases that contribute to global climate change. The provision was sponsored by Rep. Ted Poe, R-TX, a tea-party Republican who has received $273,000 in campaign contributions from the oil and gas industry since 2004, according to the Center for Responsive Politics. His district, taking in Port Arthur, Beaumont, and the Houston suburbs, has one of the largest concentrations of refineries and petrochemical plants anywhere in the world and some of the most polluted air anywhere in the country. The Texas Commission for Environmental Quality has put parts of Poe's district on an air pollutant watch list for high levels of benzene, which causes cancer; styrene, a neurotoxin; and sulfur dioxide, which attacks the respiratory system. The House approved

Poe's amendment in a 249–177 vote, with 236 Republicans in favor and 175 Democrats opposed.

- Prohibit the Environmental Appeals Board, an independent review panel within the EPA, from enforcing Clean Air Act provisions affecting oil and gas drilling projects off the coast of Alaska. The amendment was sponsored by Rep. Don Young, R-AK, who has received $1,016,463 in campaign contributions from the oil and gas industry since 1989. His provision came after the Environmental Appeals Board ruled that a Shell Oil Company proposal to drill in Arctic waters off the coast of Alaska would not meet Clean Air Act requirements, a decision that gives Shell the option of reducing its emissions to comply with the law. The House passed the amendment 243–185, with 230 Republicans supporting it and 176 Democrats opposed.

- Prohibit the EPA from enforcing a new rule to reduce the amount of mercury and other air pollution released from cement plants, and delay, upon further study, a replacement rule. The EPA estimates the rule would prevent 1,500 heart attacks, 17,000 cases of aggravated asthma and 2,500 premature deaths every year. The provision to nullify it was introduced by John Carter, R-TX, a tea party Republican who has received $467,726 in campaign contributions from the real estate and general contracting industries since 1989, according to the Center for Responsive Politics. The House passed the measure, 250–177, with 231 Republicans in favor and 170 Democrats opposed.

There were other harmful steps taken as well, including one that would stop the EPA from strengthening safeguards aimed at reducing the amount of soot, which is linked to asthma and other respiratory ills, spewed into the air from mines, smelters, cement kilns, and other industrial facilities.

In addition to those specific provisions, the spending bill called for EPA funding cuts of $3 billion for the year, roughly a third of the agency's budget. While few federal agencies were untouched in a larger effort to reduce federal spending, the EPA was singled out for a special hammering. Slashing its budget by one third would only cut federal spending by about one tenth of 1 percent. It would, though, seriously hamstring the agency's ability to develop new safeguards and enforce existing rules, which, to hear a number of lawmakers explain it, seemed to be the main point.

In February 2011, the House passed the spending bill, as amended, on a 235–189 party-line vote. Every member voting in favor of the bill was a Republican; not a single Democrat supported it.

In the following months, the House passed a number of other measures aimed at restricting the EPA's ability to strengthen air pollution prevention, while defeating provisions that could improve air quality. In June, for instance, the House defeated a measure that would reduce air pollution from offshore drilling rigs. And in October, the House voted to block new rules aimed at reducing the smog, soot, mercury, and other toxic air pollution from cement plants.

When it comes to the air pollution that undermines public health and makes life miserable for people like Andrea Roberts, no single vote of the year was more harmful than the one House members took in September 2011 in passing the "Transparency in Regulatory Analysis of Impacts On the Nation" Act of 2011, commonly called the TRAIN Act. TRAIN wreck would be more accurate. In one fell swoop, the House voted to kill or delay for years a new EPA rule aimed at reducing the pollution that drifts into places like Cleveland from nearby states and a second new standard to curtail the amount of mercury and other toxic chemicals blasted into the air around the clock by coal-fired power plants. Those two rules are exactly what is needed to make sure future generations don't suffer the way people like Andrea Roberts have. The TRAIN Act nullified both of those rules, and then made sure replacement standards would be delayed for years pending further study. The mercury and air toxics rule, by the way, has already been delayed for two decades. It was ordered under Clean Air Act amendments signed into law by President George H. W. Bush, but opposition from power plant owners and their allies in Congress have been kicking the can down the road ever since. The TRAIN Act followed in that sorry tradition.

On September 23, 2011, the House approved the TRAIN Act, 249–169, with 230 Republicans voting for the bill and 165 Democrats voting against it. Andrea Roberts summed up her reaction in two words: "Quite angry."

Then she caught her breath and continued.

"I'm almost in tears actually, because of what I've been through," she said. "I don't know how they can do that. I try to look at the big picture. But if that is the true outcome of what they've been doing, it's just unconscionable to me. I wonder about my kids, really."

THE POLLUTERS ARE WRITING THE CHECKS

A few days before Christmas 2011, a dozen Chesapeake Bay watermen gathered with Maryland officials in Annapolis to discuss how officials divvy up the state's 2 million pounds of rockfish each year among 1,130 or so commercial fishermen.

The watermen don't much like being told when and where to fish or how much they may take home. And yet, there they were, working with state regulators and playing by the rules, part of the price of doing business, several said, in an industry dependent upon the proper management of our natural resources.

That kind of fair play isn't reciprocated across much of the six-state bay watershed, where polluters get away with allowing chemicals, sediment, and other pollution to flow into the bay from the region's factories, sewage plants, parking lots, and farms. Once in the bay, these pollutants poison and cloud the water and overload it with nutrients that breed oxygen-sapping algae blooms which create giant "dead zones" where marine and plant life can't survive.

The largest estuary in the country and one of the most biologically productive anywhere in the world, the Chesapeake Bay provides a vital ecological link between the eastern Seaboard and the Atlantic Ocean, a nursery for striped bass and other deepwater fish. It was the gateway to the continent for the first permanent English settlers in America, led, in 1607, by Captain John Smith, who wrote that he and his men speared flounder in the bay with their swords, taking "more in one hour than we could eat in a day."

Named by the English for a local tribe of Native Americans, the Chesapeake Bay is fed by a watershed extending from central New York to southeastern Virginia. With a population of 17 million people, the region's commercial output and municipal waste are flushed into the watershed every day by 1,679 factories and other industrial sites, and 3,582 municipal sewage and water treatment plants.

The pollution from these and other sources has impaired water quality across 97 percent of the bay, state and federal officials report, as evidenced by low oxygen levels, poor water clarity, and other vital signs. Oysters, once a foundational presence across the bay, have been all but wiped out, with bay-wide populations estimated in 2010 at about 1 percent of historic levels. Fish kills are common and widespread, with algae blooms spreading red plumes of death across the once-fertile waters of the bay.

With so much at stake for a national treasure, veteran watermen like Don Pierce can't understand why cities, farmers, and factories are allowed to pollute the bay, while wildlife and law-abiding watermen pay the price.

"That's exactly what's happening," he said. "I think it's totally wrong."

Small wonder. Pierce lives with the toll pollution takes on the bay: crab pots that come up filled with dead crabs killed in oxygen-depleted water; oyster roasts consigned to memory; clutches of grass shrimp floating dead at the edge of the struggling marsh.

"I have seen crabs crawl out of the water, because there was no oxygen in the water, and walk up on a table or walk up on a ramp and sit there and let the sun cook them until they're dead," he explained. "It breaks your heart. It breaks your wallet. It breaks your faith in our political leaders."

Actually, Congress did pass laws meant to protect navigable waterways like the bay, beginning with 1972 legislation popularly known as the Clean Water Act. Provisions aimed at cleaning up the Chesapeake Bay date to the presidency of Ronald Reagan and were reauthorized in 2000.

Before writing rules to implement the bay clean-up provisions, the EPA performed years of scientific and economic research, to ensure that the regulations do what the law requires and that the benefits outweigh the costs. The agency held nearly 400 meetings with representatives of state and local governments, farmers, homebuilders, and others throughout the six-state bay watershed. In the fall of 2009, the EPA hosted sixteen public meetings—at locations from Williamsburg, Virginia, to Binghamton, New York—with participation from more than 2,000 citizens, to make sure the rules could be implemented in a way that works for the people of the region.

In September 2010, the agency proposed draft rules to limit the amount of phosphorus, nitrogen, and sediment flowing into the 100,000 streams and rivers that feed into the bay from across its Mid-Atlantic watershed. In the weeks that followed, the agency held more eighteen public meetings, during which more than 2,800 people responded to the rules.

Anyone who couldn't attend the public meetings could send written comments—electronically, by mail, or by hand delivery—and more than 14,000 individuals and organizations did so, including private citizens, industry groups, scholars, and others. EPA officials considered and responded to the comments, more than 90 percent of which favored the limits the EPA proposed.

Finally, at the end of December 2010, the EPA issued new rules to limit the pollution that's destroying the Chesapeake Bay. Putting the waters on what the EPA calls a "pollution diet," the agency set total maximum daily load limits on the amount of pollution that can enter the bay. The goal is a 25 percent cut in nitrogen, a 24 percent reduction in phosphorus and 20 percent lower amounts of sediment coming into the bay by 2025. In addition to improving the water quality of the nation's largest natural estuary, the limits will help restore health to tens of thousands of rivers, lakes, and streams across the Chesapeake watershed.

Total maximum daily load limits are a tried and proven tool for protecting the nation's waters, one the EPA has used in more than 40,000 other waterways nationwide. To minimize disruptions and give all parties time to accommodate needed change, the reductions are to be made over time—in this case, fifteen years—and the rules were carefully tailored to complement state plans and resources for curbing pollution.

It would be hard to find a more comprehensive, inclusive, or transparent process for creating public policy in a democratic society. The rules were mandated by law, grounded in science, based on sound economics, informed by long experience, and carefully crafted with the full participation of tens of thousands of individual citizens and interest groups. If there is a better way to pull together consensus-based protections for a natural resource of incalculable value to the nation, no one would appear to have discovered it.

In January 2011, two weeks after the EPA issued its rules, two trade associations representing the agriculture industry filed a federal law suit charging that the pollution limits were "fatally flawed" and accusing the EPA of exceeding its authority and trying to "micromanage waterways" across the region. The suit, filed in U.S. District Court in Pennsylvania by the American Farm Bureau Federation and the Pennsylvania Farm Bureau, asks that the rules be thrown out and the EPA be prohibited from "enforcing, applying or implementing" the standards.

Agriculture is big business in the bay watershed. With 87,000 farms spread out over 6.5 million acres of cropland, agriculture accounts for 22 percent of the watershed land use, contributing tens of billions of dollars to the regional economy each year.

Farms, though, are also the single largest source of bay pollution. Chemical fertilizer, manure, and other waste that runs off of fields and feed lots and into the watershed account for 44 percent of the nitrogen and phosphorus in the bay, while erosion from tilled fields contributes 65 percent of the sediment load, according to the EPA. Restoring the bay will require farmers to gradually implement measures to reduce that pollution.

And so, few were surprised in February, 2011, when U.S. Rep. Bob Goodlatte, R-VA, rose on the floor of the House of Representatives to introduce a bill that would strip out of the federal budget any funding for the enforcement or implementation of the new Chesapeake Bay clean-up rules. Goodlatte's congressional district runs the length of Virginia's Shenandoah Valley, from Roanoke northward toward Luray, taking in nearly 8,000 farms that produce more than $900 million worth of poultry, eggs, cattle, pigs, apples, and other agricultural goods each year.

It isn't only the farmers, though, that Goodlatte seeks to shield from government safeguards.

In his twenty years in Congress, Goodlatte has received $1.6 million in campaign contributions from industrial giants like Cargill Inc.,

Dean Foods, the American Meat Institute, and others in the agribusiness sector. That's about 18 percent of his total, according to the Center for Responsive Politics.

Without mentioning those interests on the floor of the House, Goodlatte rose to assail the EPA for daring to try to clean up the Chesapeake, accusing the agency of a "regulatory power grab" and of proposing "arbitrary limits" on the pollution that can flow into the bay.

"These overzealous regulations will affect everyone who lives, works, and farms in the Chesapeake Bay watershed," Goodlatte asserted, warning of dire consequences for economic growth and jobs. "I believe that each individual state, and the localities in each state, know better how to manage the state's water quality goals than the bureaucrats at the EPA."

Never mind that the states have ever and always had the authority to stop polluting the bay, with the result being its near destruction. That's why the EPA is involved in the first place—and why its role is vital.

"Clearly, this amendment is designed to, and will, unravel the current effort to finally put a limit on nutrient and sediment pollution in the Chesapeake Bay," argued Rep. Jim Moran, D-VA, during the floor debate. "If this amendment passes, it will ultimately result in a loss of thousands of fishing, crabbing and tourism jobs," Moran concluded. "Now is not the time to retreat on our commitment to restore this great estuary."

Just before ten o'clock on the night of February 18, 2011, Goodlatte's bill passed in the House, 230–195, with 222 Republicans voting for the measure and 15 voting against it. Among Democrats, 180 opposed the bill, and 8 voted for it.

As a waterman who has spent his life working the waters of the Chesapeake Bay, Don Pierce is more familiar with the ebb and flow of moonlit tides than the political currents in Washington. He doesn't need the mind of a pundit, though, to explain what happened on the floor of the House that night, or its impact on watermen like him.

"We pay the ultimate price," he said. "They're going to turn their back to the polluters, because the polluters are writing the checks."

3

IT'S NOT ABOUT JOBS . . .

The Labor Day weekend of 2011 was a bitter reminder that, while the lackluster economy was slowly improving, it didn't much feel that way to the nation's workers. Fourteen million Americans—9 percent of the workforce—were officially unemployed. Another ten million had given up looking for work or settled for part-time jobs when they needed full-time paychecks. It was the worst job market, in fact, since the presidency of Ronald Reagan, when unemployment topped 8 percent for twenty-seven straight months, peaking at 10.8 percent in the fall of 1982.

As Congress prepared to return to Washington at the end of its 2011 summer break, House Majority Leader Eric Cantor, R-VA, sent his GOP colleagues a letter entitled "Memo on Upcoming Jobs Agenda." Cantor appealed for tax cuts for businesses, but the August 29 memo focused on what he called the "Top 10 job-destroying regulations." Seven of the ten were environmental safeguards, most of them aimed at reducing air pollution from industrial incinerators and boilers and aging coal-fired power plants, "costly bureaucratic handcuffs" as Cantor referred to the measures.

"By pursuing a steady repeal of job-destroying regulations," wrote Cantor, "we can help lift the cloud of uncertainty hanging over small and large employers alike, empowering them to hire more workers."

It was a refrain House Republicans repeated over and over in the following weeks and months, each time they voted to roll back, delay, or block altogether the protections that defend our environment, safety, and health.

"It seems today that the three most feared letters to American job creators, where it used to be IRS, today those letters are EPA," Rep.

Candice Miller, R-MI, said on October 6, rising on the House floor to support a bill that would nullify new EPA rules aimed at reducing air pollution from large industrial boilers. "We have to stop all of this government overregulation that is killing jobs. Certainly, House Republicans have been trying to lift the boot of big government off the necks—off the throats—of job creators and of workers who are looking for a job."

Speaking December 2 in favor of the so-called "Regulatory Accountability Act," aimed at weakening clean air and water protections, Rep. Lamar Smith, R-TX, asserted that "Government regulation has become a barrier to economic growth and job creation."

"Faced with huge, new regulatory burdens and uncertainties about what will come next," said Smith, a tea party Texan, "employers slow down hiring, stop investing, and wait for a bill from the Obama administration."

And, five days later, freshman House member Bill Johnson, R-OH, said his constituents were "fed up with unelected bureaucrats stopping job creation and delaying true economic recovery." The answer, he said, was to support the "Regulations from the Executive in Need of Scrutiny (REINS) Act," which would allow either house of Congress to kill any major regulation just by dragging their feet on the bill for seventy days. "America's job creators are buried in red tape," said Johnson. "Enough is enough."

IT'S JUST NONSENSE

For anyone who's dropped by their state division of motor vehicles lately or struggled to complete their federal tax returns, the notion of regulatory relief has a gut-level appeal. It has special resonance to those who fondly recall Ronald Reagan's 1980 campaign pledge "to take government off the backs of the great people of this country." And no one from either party favors regulation for its own sake.

"We don't believe in overregulation, and we don't believe that regulation should be burdensome," Rep. Diana DeGette, D-CO, affirmed during a January hearing on the subject before a House subcommittee on oversight and investigations. But, she stressed, "The mantra that all regulations are inherently bad and kills jobs is wrong and dangerous."

In a year of assailing environmental safeguards as job killers, House Republicans repeatedly relied on rhetoric rather than facts. There simply isn't any evidence to support the GOP illusion of some vast regulatory regime running roughshod over personal industry and individual rights. In fact, our country depends on a sound regulatory environment, as every modern economic power does, to function in a stable and predictable way. Environmental regulations create jobs and provide additional economic benefits worth hundreds of billions of dollars each year, many times their annual compliance cost, while promoting American economic growth and competitiveness.

The Obama administration has issued environmental rules, in large part, because federal courts found that regulations issued by the previous administration were too weak. They simply didn't do the job Congress directed be done in laws already passed to help clean up our water and air. Even so, in its first two years, the Obama administration issued roughly the same number of new regulations, overall, that the George W. Bush administration issued in its first two years, according to the White House Office of Management and Budget.

No federal regulator, anywhere in this country, is above the law: U.S. regulations are grounded in law and guided by law that only Congress can create. With few exceptions—most notably for certain air quality controls—the EPA, like most other agencies, calculates, scrutinizes, and weighs the costs of its regulations against projected benefits. That analysis is performed in an open and transparent way, informed by public review and comment. It is then backstopped by separate and independent analysis by the White House Office of Management and Budget. OMB frequently pares back or blocks rules that it believes could run the risk of imposing excessive costs.

"Frankly, we're not facing a regulatory avalanche," said DeGette. "These are safeguards for the American public."

And, importantly, regulations don't kill jobs: on the contrary, responsible public oversight is essential to the health and vitality of a modern economy. Dismantling needed protections won't put Americans back to work. The argument that it will is "nonsense," according to Bruce Bartlett, who served as a senior economic adviser to President Reagan and his Republican successor, President George H. W. Bush.

"It's just nonsense. It's just made up," Bartlett told the Associated Press in October 2011.

Bartlett is a career Republican who served as deputy assistant secretary for economic policy in the U.S. Treasury Department under President George H. W. Bush and was a senior policy analyst in the Reagan White House. A former executive director of the Joint Economic Committee of Congress, Bartlett also served on the staffs of former Sen. Roger Jepsen of Iowa and U.S. Representatives Jack Kemp of New York and Ron Paul of Texas, all Republicans.

"In my opinion, regulatory uncertainty is a canard invented by Republicans that allows them to use current economic problems to pursue an agenda supported by the business community year in and year out," Bartlett wrote in an October 4, 2011, column for *The New York Times* web site. "In other words, it is a simple case of political opportunism, not a serious effort to deal with high unemployment."

When it comes to understanding jobs in America, there is no more authoritative source than the U.S. Labor Department's Bureau of Labor Statistics. For more than a century, the bureau has been the government's principal repository of workforce data. As part of its work in monitoring unemployment, the bureau keeps monthly tabs on extended mass layoffs, defined as fifty or more workers let go for thirty days or longer from a single business over a period of five weeks or less. As part of its research, the bureau asks business owners or managers the reason for the layoffs.

During 2010, the bureau recorded 1,256,606 such mass layoffs. Of those, business owners and managers themselves attributed 2,971 to government regulations and interventions of all kinds. That's about two tenths of 1 percent of all layoffs. The exact percentage—0.24 percent—compares to 0.23 percent in 2009. And it was slightly lower than the 0.36 percent figure during 2008, the final year of the Bush administration.

Government regulations, in other words, barely register when it comes to layoffs. And, to the miniscule extent regulation-attributed layoffs show up at all, they've fallen since President Obama took office. House Republicans could eliminate every single federal regulation on the books, and they would address just two tenths of 1 percent of the nation's job woes. We'd still be stuck with the other 99.8 percent of the problem because regulations don't kill jobs and doing away with them won't put Americans back to work.

"I'm hearing that the number one reason American businesses are not hiring is because of regulations. It's baloney," Rep. Jim Himes, D-CT, said on the House floor in December. Himes, who spent 12 years as a New York investment banker before being elected to Congress in 2008, called the notion that regulations kill jobs "a fraudulent idea."

Companies lay off workers, the Bureau of Labor Statistics data show, chiefly because of sluggish demand, seasonal shifts, corporate bankruptcies, and other financial and economic ills. The way to stimulate job growth is to address those concerns, not to do away with needed public safeguards.

Business surveys confirm this as well.

Nearly half of the nation's small business owners—47 percent—said their "primary motivation or reason for hiring any new employees" in 2012 would be "when revenues or sales have increased" (27 percent) or "when the economy improves" (20 percent), according to an October 2011 survey by Wells Fargo and the Gallup polling organization. Third on the list was the need to support business growth or expansion (17 percent), and fourth was replacing an employee who left (10 percent). The survey queried 604 owners of businesses having annual revenues of $20 million or less and has a margin of error of 4 percentage points.

Complying with federal rules can be a headache, certainly, whether the issue is maintaining workplace safety standards or filling out Social Security forms. As a factor in hiring decisions, though, government regulations seldom register.

A July 2011 *Wall Street Journal* survey of economists found that "the main reason U.S. companies are reluctant to step up hiring is scant demand, rather than uncertainty over government policies."

The next month, reporters from McClatchy Newspapers contacted small businesses across the country, inquiring as to whether government regulation was smothering growth.

"Their response was surprising," wrote Kevin Hall, the lead correspondent on the project. "None of the business owners complained about regulation in their particular industries, and most seemed to welcome it," Hall wrote in a story carried by newspapers across the country. "Some pointed to the lack of regulation in mortgage lending as a principal cause of the financial crisis that brought about the Great Recession of 2007–2009 and its grim aftermath."

THE SENTRIES WERE NOT AT THEIR POSTS

There's a good argument to be made, in fact, that the lack of adequate financial regulation is the single biggest job killer in American history. The 2008 financial collapse was caused, in part, by what an independent congressional commission found to be "profound lapses in regulatory oversight." Two years after the collapse, some twenty-six million Americans remained out of work or unable to find full-time jobs, four million families had lost their homes and nearly $11 billion in household wealth—mostly the value of stocks and homes—had been wiped out, devastating retirement accounts, college savings, and nest eggs of all description.

One of the main reasons for the disastrous bust was "scant regulation" of a financial system that had become similar to "a highway where there were neither speed limits nor neatly painted lines," the independent Financial Crisis Inquiry Commission found. "We conclude widespread failures in financial regulation and supervision proved devastating to the stability of the nation's financial markets," the congressionally mandated commission stated in its January 2011 report.

"The sentries were not at their posts, in no small part due to the widely accepted faith in the self-correcting nature of the markets and the ability of financial institutions to effectively police themselves," the commission reported. "More than thirty years of deregulation and reliance on self-regulation by financial institutions . . . had stripped away key safeguards that could have helped avoid catastrophe."

Lax public oversight contributed to another disaster, the 2010 BP blowout that killed eleven workers and gushed 180 million gallons of toxic crude oil into the Gulf of Mexico. There it destroyed marine life in some of the richest, most fertile fisheries anywhere in the world. It oiled more than 600 miles of coastline, wetlands, and estuaries. And it threw scores of thousands of Americans—in the fishing, hospitality, and oil industries—out of work.

"Decades of inadequate regulation" helped set the stage for the disaster as public oversight "failed to keep pace with the industrial expansion and new technology" in the offshore drilling industry, the National Commission on the BP Deepwater Horizon Oil Spill and Offshore Drilling concluded in its January 2011 report. "The result was a serious, and ultimately inexcusable, shortfall in supervision of offshore drilling," the commission found. "With the benefit of hindsight, the only question had become not whether an accident would happen but when."

And insufficient oversight of the way our food is produced, processed, transported, and prepared is one reason why the Centers for Disease Control reports that 48 million Americans get sick, 128,000 of them are hospitalized, and 3,000 die each year from salmonella, norovirus, and similar sickness.

"Preventing food-borne illness is a core public health principle that is especially critical in an increasingly complex and globalized world," U.S. Food and Drug Administration Commissioner Margaret Hamburg said in December 2010 after the toll of food-related illnesses moved Congress to pass the Food Safety Modernization Act. "Under this new law," she said, "FDA will now have new prevention-based tools, as well as a clear regulatory framework, to help make substantial improvements in our approach to food safety."

Responsible public oversight of our health, safety, economic security, and environment is as essential as the laws that govern highway traffic, workplace safety, or airline operations. We simply cannot function effectively without broad, commonsense safeguards and the confidence, certainty, and predictability they lend.

"Properly designed regulations can provide benefits by reducing damage to people's health or the environment, reducing the risks posed to the economy by the financial system, or advancing other social goals," said Douglas Elmendorf, director of the bipartisan Congressional Budget Office, in November 2011 testimony before the Senate Budget Committee.

It's not always possible to put a dollar value on the broad health benefits of clean water and air. And there's no real market that can put a price on the natural splendor and recreational pleasures of public lands and open spaces. Economists can, and do, develop models aimed at putting a price tag on these benefits. They seldom capture the true value of such intangible benefits because people don't buy them and, really, they're not for sale.

"Cost-benefit analysis is no theology. It is, instead, an effort to assist both government and citizens, in the hope of ensuring that risk regulation will actually promote its purposes," former Harvard law professor Cass Sunstein wrote in his 2002 book *Risk and Reason: Safety, Law and the Environment*, a seminal work on balancing regulatory costs and benefits. "Beaches and parks and wolves and seals are not reducible to their economic value," Sunstein wrote, cautioning that "We should not think that the monetary 'bottom line' is anything magical; it is simply a helpful input into the decision."

Despite those limitations, federal regulations are subjected to rigorous cost and benefit analysis, and they're held to a high standard. When new federal rules or regulations of major consequence are written, the agency involved usually must calculate the projected costs of the measure and estimate a value for its benefits. Agencies have been doing that for nearly twenty years.

"The American people deserve a regulatory system that works for them, not against them: a regulatory system that protects and improves their health, safety, environment, and well being and improves the performance of the economy without imposing unacceptable or unreasonable costs on society," President Bill Clinton wrote in a 1993 executive order requiring federal regulatory agencies to assess the costs, as well as the benefits, of potential new rules and standards.

In January 2011, President Obama affirmed those goals and strengthened the call to ensure that federal regulations make sense.

"Our regulatory system must protect public health, welfare, safety, and our environment, while promoting economic growth, innovation, competitiveness, and job creation," Obama wrote in an executive order. "It must be based on the best available science. It must allow for public participation and an open exchange of ideas. It must promote predictability and reduce uncertainty. It must identify and use the best, most innovative, and least burdensome tools for achieving regulatory ends. It must take into account benefits and costs, both quantitative and qualitative."

Those requirements apply to new rules or standards of any consequence issued by some thirty federal agencies, including the

Environmental Protection Agency. Economists say the studies generally overestimate the costs of environmental safeguards because they don't figure in the skill and creativity American businesses bring to the task of cleaning up pollution in a cost-effective way.

"Any bias in the government cost estimates is likely to be that of overstating the costs of environmental regulations," according to Isaac Shapiro, director of regulatory policy research at the Economic Policy Institute, a nonpartisan Washington think tank. "Among the reasons why is that cost estimates fail to account for how innovation may lead to lower compliance costs," Shapiro wrote in a November 22 blog on the costs and benefits of regulations. "Once rules are established, companies perform well at conforming to them in an efficient manner."

Beyond assessing the costs and benefits of future rules and regulations, Obama's executive order went one step further, requiring agencies to scour existing regulations—more than 165,000 pages of them—to make sure their benefits are in line with their costs. In the case of federal regulations generally, though, and EPA rules in particular, the benefits vastly exceed the costs.

How do we know? Congress requires the White House Office of Management and Budget to assess the costs and benefits of federal regulations each year. It turns out that government regulations have saved the country up to $7 trillion over the past decade, at a cost of between $44 billion and $62 billion a year, according to the 2011 annual report from the budget office. Analysts reviewed 3,325 regulations of all sorts. Environmental rules did particularly well, with air pollution standards alone making up more than 62 percent of the total benefits that could be monetized, as cleaner air means fewer deaths, hospital visits, and lost work days per year.

The air quality benefits of one new rule alone—the Mercury and Air Toxics Standards the EPA put out in December, 2011—will avert up to 17,000 premature deaths a year and thousands of heart attacks, bronchitis cases, and asthma attacks the EPA projects. That will save the country between $59 billion and $140 billion annually by 2016, the agency estimates, or between five and thirteen times more than what owners of coal burning power plants will spend to clean up the pollution they now cough up into our air.

The EPA relies on professional, peer-reviewed economic analysis for its estimates, using the same kind of accounting and projection methods employed by blue chip private firms. Still, the EPA's own cost and benefit analyses are not the last word on the matter. The work of the EPA, like that of other federal regulatory agencies, is reviewed by the White House Office of Management and Budget through the obscure yet powerful Office of Information and Regulatory Affairs.

To head the office, Obama named Sunstein, the former Harvard Law School professor who has written so extensively on the importance, and the limitations, of trying to balance the costs of regulation against its benefits. Weighing those factors, critically and effectively, is the driving force behind his work at the White House budget office.

"There are three words—cumulative cost, competitiveness, and job creation—that are very much our focus," Sunstein testified in June 2011 before the House Energy and Commerce Committee's subcommittee on Oversight and Investigations. "This is something daily we are attending to."

Critics of this approach assert that it gives corporate polluters an advantage over the interests of the public at large. Corporations are experts, after all, at assigning a dollar value to the costs of doing business. We all know there are valuable public benefits to a clean and healthy environment. It's not always possible, though, to accurately score those gains in dollars and cents. When the game is to put numbers on the table, the table naturally tilts toward the party that can master the numbers. As a result, "environmental advocates, decision makers, and citizens concerned about the environment often find themselves on the defensive," economists Frank Ackerman and Lisa Heinzerling wrote in their 2004 book *Priceless: On Knowing the Price of Everything and the Value of Nothing*, which looks at how cost and benefit analyses give corporate interests the upper hand in the political contest over regulation.

"The basic problem with narrow economic analysis of health and environmental protection is that human life, health, and nature cannot be described meaningfully in monetary terms," they wrote. "To say that life, health, and nature are priceless is not to say that we should spend an infinite amount of money to protect them. Rather, it is to say that translating life, health, and nature into dollars is not a fruitful way of deciding how much protection to give them. A different way of thinking and deciding about them is required."

In our democracy, that is largely the job of our political leaders. We depend on their judgment to help close the gap between the true value of our environment and health and what we can measure in dollars and cents. Disagreements are inevitable and often highly charged. When politicians try to scapegoat the EPA, though, and contend that environmental protections ignore economic interests, they're just plain wrong. If anything, as Ackerman and Heinzerling point out, our system of governance and our approach to cost and benefit analysis, put the ball clearly in the court of corporate polluters.

Environmentalists assailed Sunstein, for example, when the White House put the brakes on a 2011 EPA rule that would have reduced the pollution that causes ground-level ozone. The main constituent of smog, ozone can cause wheezing, chest pain, and other respiratory ills. It aggravates asthma, bronchitis, and emphysema and, with repeated exposure, can cause permanent lung damage. In September 2011, as the EPA was poised to issue a new rule to reduce ozone, Sunstein wrote a letter to the agency's administrator, Lisa Jackson, citing the need "to minimize regulatory costs and burdens, particularly in this economically challenging time." For that reason, Sunstein wrote, President Obama "has made it clear that he does not support finalizing the rule at this time."

Environmentalists were livid, accusing Obama of turning his back on air pollution to appease industry lobbyists and quiet congressional critics. The Center for Progressive Reform, a nonprofit citizens' watchdog group based in Washington, took aim at Sunstein's office, asserting that it leaned too heavily toward nixing environmental safeguards to keep from imposing outsized expense on the U.S. economy.

"No policy that might distress influential industries—from oil production to coal mining to petrochemical manufacturing—goes into effect without OIRA's approval," the center stated, using the acronym for Sunstein's office. After analyzing that office's work, the center concluded that "a stampede of industry lobbyists" met with the office's staff a staggering 3,760 times during the past decade, resulting in changes to 84 percent of the regulations proposed by the EPA.

Those changes certainly weakened environmental protections, but it's not clear they did much to create jobs. That's because, in addition to helping to keep workers healthy enough to stay on the job, cleaning up and preventing pollution itself takes work. The services and equipment required to get the job done supported a $312 billion industry in 2010, according to the *Environmental Business Journal*, which tracks the market. The industry employs an estimated 1.7 million Americans—from pipe fitters and boilermakers to consultants and engineers—involved in an array of activities from wastewater treatment to manufacturing monitoring and control gear.

The new rules the EPA announced in December to reduce mercury and other toxins from our air, for example, will affect nearly six hundred coal-fired power plants across the country, about 40 percent of which lack advanced pollution equipment. Building and installing the scrubbers and other gear needed to clean up the emissions from those plants will create 46,000 temporary construction jobs and full-time work for another 8,000 permanent employees, the EPA estimates.

Many of these plants will also be upgraded to reduce the air pollution that drifts across state lines, as provided for in another new EPA rule. All combined, this work will create the equivalent of 325,305 year-long jobs, according to a study by the University of Massachusetts' Political Economy Research Institute.

"We have to hire plumbers, electricians, painters; folks who do that kind of work when you retrofit a plant," Mike Morris, chief executive officer of American Electric Power Co., said of an aging coal-fired power plant in Ohio that was being equipped with modern equipment to reduce the air pollution the facility sends to states downwind. "Jobs are created in the process, no question about that," Morris told *The Washington Post* in an article that ran in November 2011.

While the House majority portrays the EPA as aloof and out of touch with the concerns of business, the agency itself listens closely to companies like American Electric Power and works hard to address real issues.

In February 2012, for example, the company's chief executive officer, Nick Akins, told investors that American Electric Power would spend $400 million to clean up mercury and other air toxins from the emissions of its coal-fired power plants in Ohio. Investors were pleased.

That was, after all, nearly two-thirds less than the $1.1 billion the company had earlier estimated for the clean-up. The difference? After listening carefully to the power company's concerns, the EPA modified its mercury and air toxins rule to accommodate industry requirements. The changes allowed the industry to use lower-cost pollution control equipment to get the job done.

U.S. expertise in environmental technologies, in fact, has enabled American workers to succeed in overseas markets as well, creating a U.S. trade surplus in environmental equipment and services. In 2009 the *Environmental Business Journal* reported that the country exported $40.5 billion worth of environmental goods and services, $13 billion more than American companies imported.

"The United States is regarded as a world leader in many ET (environmental technology) categories, including: engineering, design, construction, and consulting services; pollution prevention and resource recovery; water and wastewater handling and treatment equipment," and other areas, the U.S. Commerce Department's International Trade Administration reports in an industry fact sheet. The office estimated the global market for environmental technologies hit $800 billion in 2008 and continues to grow. "The U.S. ET industry should be able to increase its global competitiveness as it focuses great attention on key international markets and introduces new, state-of-the-art products and services."

Despite the mounting growth in job creation driven by environmental protections, many House Republicans spent 2011 making the false claim that environmental regulations were destroying jobs and undermining economic recovery. It's just not true. Regulations play virtually no role in job layoffs, exhaustive data from the Bureau of Labor Statistics show and independent business surveys verify. Impact on industry and jobs is a central consideration when new regulations are drafted. President Obama ordered all agencies to assess the economic effects of existing regulations, as well, with an eye toward eliminating any that impose excessive costs on our businesses. The agency calculations are reviewed separately by an independent White House office, which frequently pares back new environmental rules and sometimes blocks them altogether. And that office has been roundly criticized by environmentalists for bending over backward to accommodate businesses at the expense of our environment and health. The fact is environmental regulations promote job creation, predictability, and sound growth, even as they provide health benefits worth hundreds of billions of dollars each year.

"We all remember 'too big to fail.' This pseudo jobs plan to protect polluters might well be called 'too dirty to fail,'" EPA Administrator Lisa Jackson told students at the University of Wisconsin in November 2011. If House leaders prevail in rolling back environmental safeguards, she said, "the result will be more asthma, more respiratory illness, and more premature deaths. What there won't be is any clear path to new jobs."

4

. . . IT'S ABOUT PROFITS

For four decades, corporate polluters and their congressional allies have issued doomsday predictions that come down to this: cleaning up pollution will tank the economy. It isn't true; it never was.

In 1970, President Richard M. Nixon established the Environmental Protection Agency and began laying the foundations of our modern environmental laws. In the following decade, years 1971–1980, the U.S. economy grew at an average rate of 3.2 percent per year, adjusted for inflation. In 1990, when President George H. W. Bush signed the amendments that strengthened the Clean Air Act, some members of his cabinet warned that the new protections would cause a depression. And yet, after stumbling the next year in the wake of a real estate collapse linked to massive failures in the savings and loan industry, the economy picked up steam, averaging 3.4 percent growth from 1991 to 2000.

Since the dawn of effective environmental protections in 1970, in fact, the total value of goods and services the U.S. economy kicks out each year has risen from $1 trillion in 1970 to $15.3 trillion in 2011. Corporate profits, too, have flourished, growing from $83 billion in 1970 to a record $2 trillion in 2011. Many factors influence economic growth and corporate success. Looking at the record, though, it's clear that, during the decades when we've made historic progress in cleaning up our environment, American companies have prospered and our economy has thrived.

That hasn't kept some companies from claiming that regulations are forcing them to fail. It's very seldom true.

During last year's GOP rampage against our environment, Rep. Ed Whitfield, R-KY, and others who go to bat for big coal companies, advocated for a bill in October to block new limits on pollution from cement plants, which burn huge amounts of coal. "Evidence shows that

20,000 jobs are at jeopardy and 18 percent of cement plants in America may very well be closed because of this regulation," Whitfield said. He is correct that the cement industry is reeling, but no one with knowledge of the field attributes the troubles to environmental protections. The 2009 recession brought housing and office construction to a crawl, sending cement demand to its lowest level in nearly three decades. The industry itself projects it will take several more years for industry sales to recover to pre-recession levels.

In March 2011, Randy Stilley, the president of Seahawk Drilling, published an op-ed in *The Washington Post* asserting that his offshore drilling services company had failed because of federal regulations issued in the wake of the 2010 BP blowout in the Gulf of Mexico. In fact, the company's business had gone dry and more than half of its drill rigs were idle before the Deepwater Horizon disaster. Seahawk's biggest customer was the government of Mexico, which was not affected by U.S. government actions and had decided, for its own reasons, not to renew its contracts with Seahawk. Three weeks before the BP blowout, the company had warned investors it might not have enough cash to continue operations.

It's an old story. During President George W. Bush's first term, California utility companies warned that the state would face electrical brownouts because applications for new power plant permits were being held up over clean air regulations. Former New Jersey Gov. Christine Todd Whitman, who was Bush's EPA administrator at the time, met with utility officials to address their concerns.

"I said 'Fine, show me the applications that have been held up by regulation and we'll fast-track them,'" she recalled in a telephone interview. "Nobody came back with any." Instead, she learned, utilities were holding back on investment decisions based on a combination of factors, including general economic uncertainty. "It was companies deciding they weren't going to invest."

WHEN RECORD PROFITS DON'T GROW JOBS

None of this is to argue that pollution controls don't impose costs on individual polluters or that those costs shouldn't be taken into account. They do, they should and they are. It's wrong, though, to block needed oversight and improvement on the false premise that doing so will create jobs. It won't. What it does is increase polluter profits, at the expense of the environment and public safety and health.

Invariably, though, corporate polluters and their congressional allies assert that less regulation translates into job growth, as the Republican Study Committee contended in April 2011. In a fact sheet entitled "Honest Solutions," the committee, chaired by Rep. Jim Jordan, R-OH, promised to slash taxes and regulations in a way that "gets the government out of the way so American businesses have the ability to grow and create jobs."

In other words, they claim that the less our government taxes and regulates business, the more jobs business will create. If that were true, we wouldn't be in the worst job market in three decades; we'd be undergoing the biggest job boom in history.

Corporations express success in profits, and corporate profits in this country hit $1.977 trillion in 2011, according to the U.S. Bureau of Economic Analysis. That's an all-time high, both in dollars and as a percentage of the country's economic output, as measured by gross domestic product.

During the twenty years between 1990 and 2009, corporate profits, before taxes, averaged 9.3 percent of GDP. During 2011, the figure was 13 percent, the highest on record, dating back to at least 1947. That's a difference of 3.7 percentage points. On our $15.3-trillion economy, that's worth $566 billion.

That money could put a lot of people to work, if, as the GOP thinking goes, companies use additional cash to create jobs. That's not, though, how it works. For the most part, companies hire workers for one of two reasons: to meet or create growing demand for their product.

With prospects for demand growth uncertain, companies have only barely increased hiring; they have used record profits to bank record levels of cash instead. By October 2011, U.S. corporations had $2.1 trillion in cash on hand, U.S. Treasury Department data show, more than at any other time in history.

Let's be clear. Profits are vital; without them, companies can't survive. And banking cash might make strategic sense in times of middling growth. No one should be misled, however, into believing that we can somehow magically create jobs by turning our backs on the commonsense safeguards we all depend on to protect our environment and health. That simply isn't how it works.

Environmental regulations don't create pollution or the costs of dealing with it; they simply require that the polluters pay those costs, not the public. Corporate polluters don't like that, not because it impacts jobs, but because it requires them to become more efficient or see their profits fall. Period.

For the overall economy, though, making polluters pay, instead of the public, produces a huge net benefit: a healthier and more productive society and workforce, with the increased value measured in the hundreds of billions of dollars each year, including jobs created by cleaning up and reducing pollution.

Some of the industries that produce pollution as a byproduct of their operations expect the public to pay for that pollution, through dirty water, for example, poisoned air, loss of arable lands, health problems, missed work days, mental impairment, or premature deaths. Many companies got away with it for decades; some are getting away with it still. Environmental protections, though, call for the corporations that create the pollution to pay the cost of reducing it or mitigating its impact, goals we set, as a nation, two generations ago.

"We can no longer afford to consider air and water common property, free to be abused by anyone without regard to the consequences," President Nixon said in his 1970 State of the Union address. "Instead, we should begin now to treat them as scarce resources, which we are no more free to contaminate than we are free to throw garbage into our neighbor's yard."

As Nixon put it, "This requires new regulations. It also requires that, to the extent possible, the price of goods should be made to include the costs of producing and disposing of them without damage to the environment."

That's not just good governance; it's common sense. It's also, as it happens, sound economics.

"Environmental pollution poses a problem for the economy," the bipartisan Congressional Budget Office (CBO) wrote in a 1988 report entitled "Assessing the Costs of Environmental Legislation."

"Absent corrective policies, polluters—whether the owners of factories or the operators of motor vehicles—have little incentive to stop polluting because the costs are borne by others while the polluters themselves profit," the CBO explained. "As long as the costs created by pollution remain 'external' to the polluter, society effectively subsidizes polluters and their activities."

When corporate polluters and their congressional allies jump up and down about the so-called costs of environmental regulations, in other words, they're actually arguing for more public subsidies for corporations and their shareholders. They're arguing in favor of a form of corporate welfare. They're arguing against the free market. What a free market does, after all, is to assign value to production, through costs, and to signal, through prices, how much the fruits of that production are worth. A system that allows producers to shift costs to the public is not a free market; it's a free ride for corporate shareholders, at the expense of the public good. That's inefficient, in economic terms. And it's contrary to the pursuit of equity, justice, and fairness in a democratic society.

The goal of responsible environmental safeguards is simply to require of corporate polluters exactly what we ask of every kindergarten student anywhere in the country: when you make a mess, you clean it up. When polluters pay the price of their pollution, it makes our economy more efficient, not less. That's because it allows the market to assign a fair value, not just to the benefits of production, but also to the costs that went into it, including pollution costs otherwise forced upon the public.

"If regulation reflects the extent of these external costs, it can lead all economic actors to incorporate the true costs and consequences of their activities into their economic decision making and, therefore, improve the well-being that society derives from its resources," the CBO report states.

And that allows the market to more efficiently sort out winners and losers.

"Production of goods and services that lead to pollution will contract, and with it employment and affluence in some communities or regions," the CBO asserts. "At the same time, production of substitutable goods and services, and of goods and services used in abating pollution, will increase."

Polluters may howl; they have that right. But the public good must win out. That's the point of democracy. And the public wins, and wins big, when corporations are held accountable for the pollution they create.

5

PUTTING THE
NATION AT RISK

During 2011, the country struggled with historic debt and the lingering fallout from the worst recession in six decades. U.S. troops fought for a tenth grinding year in Afghanistan and finally came home from Iraq after eight years of fighting there. Financial crisis upon crisis rolled across Europe, shaking the continent's common currency and driving American allies like Italy, Greece, Ireland, and others to the brink of economic collapse. Much of the explosive Middle East was remade in unpredicted and unpredictable ways by power-to-the-people street revolutions that eventually reached the gates of the Kremlin. And income inequality worldwide turned Occupy Wall Street into a global movement.

As turmoil, challenge, and opportunity combined to roil our nation and our world during anxious months of ferment and change, which of these pressing issues commanded the attention of the U.S. House of Representatives? Putting our fiscal house in order? Defeating our battlefield foes? Shoring up our trans-Atlantic partners and friends? Bolstering the fragile beginnings of democracy abroad? Addressing the yawning gap between rich and poor?

What single action, in fact, did the Republican-led House take during the course of the year that might have the faintest influence over any of those boiling concerns or our nation's ability to cope with them? Nothing quickly comes to mind—the principal reason the Congress ended the year with its lowest job approval rating in history. In late December, as Congress wrapped up what *The Washington Post* called "one of its least productive sessions in recent memory," just 11 percent of the American people approved of the job legislators had done, according to the Gallup Organization. By February 2012, support had fallen to 10 percent—yet another record low—despite the exceptional challenges and opportunities Americans were looking to our lawmakers to address.

What the House majority did instead was to muster its indignation and political will to wage the single greatest legislative assault in history against the foundational protections we all depend on to defend our environment and health. Was there really no better way for House members to spend their time than to stand up day after day, debate after debate, and take one vote after another to target the world we live in and the future we share?

In the best of times, this dangerous and destructive campaign would put our resources, our children, and our country at risk. In this year, in these times, this legislative offensive imperiled the country in extraordinary ways. We will never know the price we will pay for the problems that got kicked down the road unsolved, the opportunities left on the table, and the challenges put off for another day by a Congress that chose to focus on targeting our environment instead. Without question, though, the decision to squander the 2011 House agenda to impose havoc on our environmental safeguards has posed special dangers, for three important reasons.

First, we're in the opening stages of an epic domestic oil and gas boom. It has the potential to transform our lands, our waters, our air, and our communities as thoroughly as it infuses our economy. This is no time to back down from our national commitment to a clean environment and public health or to back away from the professionals we rely on to enforce needed safeguards. Now is the time to make sure they're up to the risks that are mounting before us. Irreparable harm awaits our nation if we fail.

Second, converging with this fossil fuel boom, there is a clean energy revolution sweeping the country and, for that matter, the world. It has already attracted $1 trillion in investments worldwide. It has put millions of Americans back to work and promises to create jobs for millions more. Legions of carpenters, electricians, engineers, and others already go to work each day doing things like developing and installing wind, solar, and other renewable power sources and building the energy-efficient cars, homes, and workplaces of tomorrow. They are competing for sales in a global clean energy bazaar worth hundreds of billions of dollars each year. In this high-stakes contest for the jobs of the future, we can't afford to put our workers at a disadvantage while rivals in China, Germany, and other countries are given the tools they need to succeed.

Finally, the demands that growth and industrialization are placing on our world mean that time is running out for us to put in place the forward-leaning policies that will safeguard our resources for future generations and protect us all from further harm. Americans understand the stakes. They are solidly behind the need for us to get this right. Our political leaders owe it to their constituents, and to the country, to act, speak, and vote in ways that faithfully represent the deep-seated values that have long supported a national consensus.

"Clean air and water, productive and beautiful lands, abundant wildlife and plentiful energy and natural resources are part of America's heritage," President Ronald Reagan said in a 1987 message to Congress. "Throughout history, Americans have sustained a deep, abiding relationship with their land and a reverence for this natural resource heritage," he said. "And the vast majority of Americans today hold similar values."

U.S. DEPENDENCY ON FOREIGN OIL FALLS

Those American values are what we elect our leaders to uphold—in the White House and the Congress. Unfortunately, what we got instead during 2011 was a sad and sorry trail of distortions and misrepresentations from the House majority, beginning with the great false myth of our energy future.

"Since President Obama has taken office, American energy production has been halted and the average national price of gasoline has doubled," the House majority party stated in its mid-year report titled, "The House Republican Plan for America's Job Creators." States the GOP report, "The rising price of gasoline and dependence on foreign oil means less money for families struggling to make ends meet and for business owners who are trying to get our economy moving again."

That statement was a far cry from the truth.

American energy production halted? No, it's booming. Gasoline prices and dependence on foreign oil rising? Not so. Let's take a look at the facts, as documented by the U.S. Department of Energy's data and analysis arm, the U.S. Energy Information Administration, the most authoritative source for this kind of information anywhere in the world.

First, as to prices and imports.

Gasoline prices peak each year at the height of the summer driving season. In July 2008, six months before Obama took office, regular gasoline averaged $4.05 per gallon nationwide. That's the highest price Americans had ever paid, and it happened while President George W. Bush, a former Texas oilman, was in office.

The following July, Obama's first summer as president, gasoline averaged $2.54 a gallon. In July 2010, the price was $2.74. And in July 2011, as Middle East upheaval and measured world recovery drove crude oil prices upward, gasoline rose to $3.65 a gallon, higher than in previous months, to be sure, but still lower than the record set on Bush's watch.

By March 2012—nearly a year after the House GOP report—prices were again approaching $4.00 a gallon. The reason was rising crude oil prices due to growing global demand and uncertainty over supplies as a result of international sanctions imposed on Iran to try to keep that country's alleged nuclear weapons ambition in check.

Little wonder, then, most Americans don't buy the GOP charge that Obama is somehow to blame for high gasoline prices. The majority—60 percent—blame the oil companies or the oil-exporting nations, according to a May 2011 survey conducted jointly by Republican and Democratic polling outfits for George Washington University and Politico. In that poll, which queried 1,000 likely voters nationwide, only 12 percent blamed Obama for high oil prices, while 11 percent said prices were rising because of measured economic recovery.

The truth is that presidents, Republican or Democrat, have only so much impact on gasoline prices. Crude oil prices—set on a world market—account for about two thirds of the cost of motor gasoline, which makes up nearly half of all the oil we use.

"This notion that a politician can wave a magic wand and impact the 90-million-barrel-a-day global oil market is preposterous," Paul Bledose, strategic adviser to the Bipartisan Policy Center, told *The Washington Post* in an article published in March 2012.

What Obama has done is to reach a historic agreement with car manufacturers to increase the mileage our cars get from each gallon we buy. That will reduce gasoline demand, which can bring prices down. And, by helping to squeeze more from each gallon of gas, it will save consumers billions of dollars at the pump each year, no matter what happens to gas prices.

In 1991, American passenger cars old and new averaged 21.1 miles per gallon. By 2008, the figure was 22.6 miles per gallon, an improvement of just 0.9 percent. In the quest to build more fuel-efficient cars, we lost twenty years, under Democratic and Republican presidents alike.

In July 2011, after extensive talks with the Obama administration—and over the objections of House Republicans—the makers of cars and light trucks agreed to improve their new vehicle fleet average to 54.5 miles per gallon beginning with the 2025 model year. The difference will save Americans $80 billion a year at the pump and reduce our oil use by 3.1 million barrels per day by 2030, the White House projects. It will cut automobile carbon emissions in half. And it will create up to 150,000 American jobs, as Detroit shows the world how to build the next generation of fuel-efficient vehicles.

At 18.8 million barrels a day, U.S. oil consumption remained the world's highest in 2011. We import nearly half of our supply. That's a problem that drains our economy of needed resources, to the tune of roughly $1 billion a day, while putting our national security at risk and putting in harm's way the men and women who protect us and our oil supplies around the world.

U.S. oil use has fallen, though, by 9.5 percent since our 2005 peak. That's partly because Americans have begun showing a preference for more fuel-efficient cars and even hybrids that can run on electricity. In the spring of 2011, 61 percent of Americans said they would "seriously consider getting a more fuel-efficient car" the next time they bought one, according to a CNN-Opinion Research Corp. poll of 1,034 adults nationwide. The new fuel efficiency standards are designed to help General Motors, Ford, Chrysler, and other car makers provide consumers with more fuel-saving choices in a way that responds to changing attitudes. Those shifting preferences are a big reason why U.S. dependence on petroleum imports has been falling for half a decade.

In 2011, we imported 11.4 million barrels per day of crude oil and refined fuels. That's the lowest level since 1999, and it's down 12 percent since Obama took office. We exported, in 2011, 2.9 million barrels a day of diesel fuel, jet fuel, and other refined products. That's an all-time high and 59 percent more than we shipped out in 2008.

The bottom line: With imports down and exports up, we purchased, on balance, 8.5 million barrels of imported oil and petroleum products per day. On a net basis, we relied on foreign supplies for about 45 percent of our petroleum needs in 2011, down from 60 percent just five years before. That's progress, and we need to keep at it.

THE DOMESTIC OIL AND GAS BOOM

What about that so-called halt in domestic energy production? That's the biggest whopper yet.

During 2011, companies drilled 23,503 new oil wells in this country. That's 42 percent more than in 2010 and more than double the number drilled during 2009, President Obama's first year in office. It's more, by far, than were drilled in any year during the George W. Bush administration; more, in fact, than in any year since the mid-1980s, according to the U.S. Energy Information Administration.

Not only are we drilling for oil at a robust clip, we're also finding it. Domestic oil production hit 5.9 million barrels per day by the end of 2011. That's 18.4 percent higher than Bush's last year in office and the highest level, overall, since 1999. Similarly, in 2011 natural gas production in this country rose to a record 28 trillion cubic feet for the year. That's up 10 percent since 2008 and 20 percent since 2005.

The double-digit jump in output reflects a domestic drilling boom, mostly in underground shale deposits where huge amounts of oil and gas are trapped. With extensive assistance from the Department of Energy, the oil and gas industry has developed new drilling technologies and methods that are enabling companies to tap shale deposits from North Dakota to Texas and from Pennsylvania to California.

The availability of this shale resource has dramatically increased the country's estimated crude oil and natural gas reserves, a measure of how much is thought to be in the ground and able to be produced. The shale deposits have brought our latest estimates of natural gas reserves to a staggering 2.2 quadrillion cubic feet. That's the equivalent of a 92-year supply at current consumption levels. Shale finds have as much as doubled our estimates of U.S. crude oil reserves, bringing that to roughly 45 billion barrels, about 3.4 percent of the world total.

Extracting oil and gas from underground shale, though, presents grave environmental risks that have rattled communities nationwide. The safeguards we need to do this right have lagged far behind the breakneck pace of industry drilling.

Tapping shale depends on two industrial operations—hydraulic fracturing, or "fracking," and underground horizontal drilling—that can threaten air quality, surface and ground water supplies, and even the stability of bedrock formations deep underground.

To break gas or oil loose from shale, producers drill a hole, sometimes a mile deep or more, to get to the fuel-rich shale. Then they drill horizontally along the deposit. Into that hole they then inject huge amounts of water—typically a million gallons or more per well—laced with a witch's brew of industrial chemicals, some of which are toxic or can cause cancer. This fracking fluid, as it's called, is blasted in at high pressure that shatters the shale, releasing the gas or oil.

Most of the fluid remains underground. There, under certain conditions, it can contaminate ground water supplies. The fluid that returns to the surface contains the industrial chemicals that went down the shaft as well as salts and even radioactive material the earth burps back up. That fluid is potentially hazardous to the environment, wildlife, and human health. In some states, though, it is dumped into holding ponds, where it's often a disaster waiting to burst or leak, or it's released into regional rivers and streams after treatment in area water facilities that are seldom equipped to properly treat such waste.

State and federal agencies have blamed fracking for contaminated wells in Pennsylvania, Wyoming, and other parts of the country. A British company said in November 2011 that its fracking operations likely caused a series of earthquakes in Lancashire earlier in the year. And scientists are reviewing possible links between fracking and earthquakes in several U.S. states, including Ohio, Oklahoma, Texas, and Arkansas.

Fracking also brings convoys of large trucks into communities where drilling takes place. Diesel fumes and road dust choke the air as trucks haul in equipment, pipes, water, chemicals, and other supplies. And fracking, by its nature, releases large amounts of methane—a powerful greenhouse gas—into the atmosphere.

Public oversight hasn't kept pace with the fracking boom. In some cases, needed protections have been intentionally undermined.

As fracking's potential began to emerge several years ago, Congress exempted the practice from key environmental safeguards, such as the Clean Water Act and the Safe Drinking Water Act. That left the Environmental Protection Agency with few tools to ensure that fracking doesn't damage our environment and health. That needs to change—and the sooner the better.

In his January 2012 State of the Union address, Obama said he would order companies that drill for gas on public lands to disclose the chemicals they use in, for example, fracking fluid, vowing that "America will develop this resource without putting the health and safety of our citizens at risk."

That's an important start, but it's only a first step. Most fracking is currently taking place on private property, not public lands, and the public deserves to know what chemicals are being used on private property wells.

We also should put watersheds and other environmentally critical or sensitive regions off-limits to the risks of fracking. We need to set clean air standards that target methane leaks from wells. We must hold operators to the highest drilling and construction standards and treat toxic residue from oil and gas operations as the hazardous waste that it is. State and federal agencies need adequate funding to enforce fracking safeguards. And we need national policies that encourage the most efficient and responsible use of the gas and oil we produce, from fracking or any other method.

Unless and until we have needed safeguards and policies in place, along with the people and resources to enforce them, it's irresponsible to race ahead with this perilous practice. Now is the time to make sure that we do this properly, or not at all. We won't have a second chance to get this right. We need people of good will, from both political parties, to do that, or we will continue to put our future at risk.

A $3 TRILLION MARKET

The new domestic oil and gas boom is playing out against the background of a second historic energy revolution, fueled by renewable power and efficiency gains. Here, too, we need responsible public policies to ensure that we make the most of this chance to strengthen our economy, make our country more secure, and create a healthier future for our children.

There are few national imperatives more urgent for our country than developing the safe, clean, and sustainable energy sources that will power us into the twenty-first century. Harnessing power from the sun and the wind must be part of the mix.

We've made a strong beginning. During the first eleven months of 2011, wind turbines generated 2.9 percent of our electricity. That's a small but significant contribution. It's grown 48 percent just since 2009, and it made up a third of all new electricity generating capacity during 2011, according to the Energy Information Administration. About 90,000 Americans now make their living from wind turbines.

We're getting much less electricity from solar power—less than 1 percent of our consumption—but, again, it's growing fast. It's doubled since 2009. Over the coming decade, it will grow to triple its current level, the Energy Information Administration projects.

This isn't George Jetson stuff. Wind, solar, and other renewable power sources are putting Americans to work today on the energy solutions of tomorrow, and the stakes for the country are high. We get 43 percent of our electricity from large coal-fired power plants. Scores of those are aging and will be either refitted or retired in the years to come. Obama has set a national goal of reducing coal's portion of our electricity supply to 20 percent or less by 2035. Renewable power can help replace those plants without the air pollution and health problems they cause.

In 2011, the United States led the world in clean energy investments. We installed a record $56 billion worth of equipment: solar, wind, and other renewable power gear, as well as advanced batteries and electrical lines to help store and distribute the juice, according to a January report by Bloomberg New Energy Finance, a news and data analysis service. China was close behind, investing $47.4 billion in similar equipment. Together, the two countries led clean energy investment worldwide, which hit a record $260 billion in 2011—up 5 percent above the year before and nearly five times as much as in 2004, the Bloomberg analysis shows.

Assuming even modest growth, the global market for clean energy technologies will be worth more than $3 trillion over the coming decade. Competition for that money, and the millions of jobs it will support, will be global and it will be fierce. In such a contest, second-best won't be good enough, especially not for American workers. We've already glimpsed what it can look like to lose ground.

It was American scientists who invented the photovoltaic cell in 1954 to make electricity from sunlight. For decades, we led the world in producing these cells, but in recent years we've fallen behind tough competitors in China. A come-from-behind solar juggernaut, China produced few photovoltaic cells five years ago. Today Chinese producers control half the world market. The Chinese government rightly sees solar power as a strategic industry. In 2009, Beijing provided subsidies worth an estimated $30 billion to its four largest solar panel makers, boosting their export prospects while assuring them the lion's share of China's huge and growing domestic market.

China is providing similar support for its rapidly expanding wind turbine industry, already among the world's largest. Other countries, including Germany, have had policies in place for more than a decade to promote the development of renewable power like solar and wind. Obama has vowed continued support to help U.S. firms compete.

"We're not going to cede the wind energy or the solar industry or the battery industry to China or Germany because we're too timid to make that same commitment here in the United States," Obama said in a January 2012 speech at Buckley Air Force Base in Aurora, Colorado. "We've got to double down on a clean energy industry that's never been more promising, and Congress is going to need to act."

In the past, under Democrats and Republicans alike, Congress has done just that, approving tax breaks, loan guarantees, and other incentives to help support innovative clean energy technologies. These incentives, though, need to be renewed.

Since 1992, for example, we've had a production tax credit in place that has been especially helpful to wind turbine development. The credit, though, is set to expire at the end of 2012. A federal cash grant program that has helped spur solar power growth expired at the end of 2011. President George W. Bush put in place a federal loan program in 2005 to help support clean energy growth, and Obama expanded the program as part of the 2009 economic stimulus package that Congress approved. As a result, the Department of Energy is administering some $36 billion worth of loan guarantees to help finance clean energy growth. That program, however, is fully subscribed. It stopped reviewing new offers in September 2011.

Obama has asked Congress to pass new clean energy tax credits and other incentives to help promote renewable power. Instead, House Republicans spent much of 2011 voting to cut funding for similar supports. "Every year, we have spent untold billions on these programs, and every year, we have become more dependent on foreign oil," Rep. Tom McClintock, R-CA, said in April 2011, as the House voted to slash funding for projects to promote renewable power and energy efficiency.

McClintock, of course, was wrong. We're becoming less dependent on foreign oil, partly because of public investments in efficiency gains. McClintock, though, was simply doing what his GOP colleagues in the House did all year long, politicizing an important national goal and demonizing our president for trying his best to attain it. The impact of undercutting U.S. momentum in clean energy technologies, however, goes well beyond politics.

"This unprecedented assault on the environment has devastating consequences for our economy," Rep. Gerry Connolly, D-VA, said in a House speech in September 2011. "We cannot afford to let China and Germany dominate industries such as clean technology."

The House effort to lambast clean energy supports reached its high water mark in September, when the California solar panel maker Solyndra declared bankruptcy. Before it failed, Solyndra received $535 million in federal loan guarantees under the U.S. Department of Energy's renewable power support program. With the Energy Department's help, Solyndra bet its future on an advanced technology meant to exploit its competitors' heavy reliance on silicon. Prices for silicon-based photovoltaic cells fell sharply, however, during 2010 and 2011. That was good news for consumers, but it left Solyndra with a premium-priced product in a fire-sale market, conditions that took a toll on solar companies, not only in this country, but in Europe and

Asia as well. Solyndra shuttered its spanking new factory and laid off about 1,000 workers.

With taxpayer money at risk, federal investigators launched an inquiry into possible wrongdoing. After more than six months of investigations, no misdeeds had been found. If any is, those responsible should be held to account and the Energy Department should learn the hard lessons of the loss.

That doesn't mean, though, we should turn our back, as a nation, on the promise of solar power. It's certainly no reason to give up on public support for renewable energy and efficiency gains. That, though, is exactly how a number of House Republicans responded to the Solyndra experience.

"We can't compete with China to make solar panels and wind turbines," tea party Republican Cliff Stearns of Florida told NPR in a story that aired in October 2011. As chairman of the House Energy and Commerce Committee's subcommittee on oversight and investigations, Stearns led a months-long series of hearings on the Solyndra losses, which he termed, at one point, "our own modern day great train robbery."

Others pounced on Solyndra's failings as evidence that the country is better off sticking with oil and gas than investing in renewable power. "I'm one of those that believe we should end all of these subsidy programs," Rep. Marsha Blackburn, R-TN, told Fox News in October 2011. "What we don't want is the federal government micromanaging," said Blackburn, a member of the Energy and Commerce Committee. "All these alternative energy programs and ideas, if they're good ideas, take them to the marketplace, secure your investors, then make it a profitable venture. But we know the best energy policy for the United States is going to be 'Drill here, drill now.'"

Setting aside the oil and gas boom that has sent drilling to its highest level in three decades, that argument ignores two essential facts.

First, American taxpayers have been subsidizing our energy industry for decades. Without federal subsidies, there wouldn't be a nuclear power industry. It was created by the federal government under what was called the "atoms for peace" initiative when Republican President Dwight Eisenhower sought a civilian use for technology the U.S. military developed to make nuclear bombs. Every nuclear plant in America continues to receive huge public subsidies in the form of catastrophy insurance, because the risk is too high for any private insurer to underwrite it without liability limits and no nuclear facility would operate without it. The production, transportation, and storage of the uranium that fuels such plants are overseen by the Department of Energy to prevent potential weapons material from falling into the wrong hands. The oil and gas industry receives special tax breaks worth more than $4 billion a year, according to the White House Office of Management and Budget. These are the same big oil companies that pocketed more than $130 billion in profits during 2011 alone.

In other words, taxpayers should continue subsidizing the nuclear power industry after sixty years and chip in to help out an industry that makes $1 billion in profit every three days, but we should not support emerging technologies that promise to deliver clean, sustainable domestic energy for the twenty-first century? It's hard to improve on the way Rep. Anna Eshoo, D-CA, described that approach during a House debate in April: "They are sitting in a car looking in the rearview mirror—and they think they see the future."

There's something else the GOP argument against public support for clean energy technologies ignores. We have a long history, as Americans, of pulling together to get things done. We each do our part to support national goals. That's not micromanaging; it's what makes our country strong. It's how we won World War II. It's how we won the Cold War. It's how we built the interstate highway system, the greatest public universities in the world, and the Internet. It's how we put a man on the moon, harnessing the efforts of some 400,000 Americans working through more than 20,000 companies and universities nationwide in support of the Apollo program.

"Apollo enriched our intellectual and economic life and awakened us to mankind's boundless horizon," President Ronald Reagan said during a 1984 White House ceremony marking the fifteenth anniversary of the lunar landing. "There's never a time when we can stop moving forward, when we can stop dreaming," Reagan said. "The footprints on the Moon showed us that America's future can be determined by our dreams and our visions."

This is no time to stop moving forward, especially when we know that a thriving renewable power industry will create jobs, make our companies more competitive, cut our energy costs, and reduce the pollution that puts us all at risk. Those are national goals that will benefit Americans everywhere. They deserve our collective support. That's why 83 percent of Americans favor public incentives for solar and other alternative power sources, according to a *USA Today*/Gallup poll taken in January 2011. What more than eight Americans out of every ten seem to understand is that public money can help bridge the gap between what private investors are willing to risk and what is required to give emerging technologies and the workers who build them a fighting chance to succeed.

Not every new idea will pan out; not every new company will make the cut—most Americans understand that too. But when we struggle, when we fail, the answer is not to give up on the promise of clean energy or shrug off the loss of opportunity and jobs. Rather, we step up our game, learn the lessons of our failure, and come back stronger the next time. At least, that's what we've done around here for the past couple centuries or so.

"We need you to dream big," President Obama said in a March 2012 speech in Nashua, New Hampshire. "We need you to summon the same spirit of unbridled optimism, that bold willingness to tackle tough problems that led previous generations to meet the challenges of their time—to power a nation from coast to coast, to touch the moon, to connect the entire world with our own science and imagination. That's what America's capable of doing. And it's that history that teaches us that all of our challenges, all of them, are within our power, with our grasp, to solve."

We won't get the job done by trying to score political points and maligning those leaders who see renewable power as part of a broader mix of promising energy technologies that can strengthen our nation's future. And we won't get where we need to go by continuing to put polluters first and forgoing the needed standards and commonsense safeguards that protect our environment and our health in ways that also promote the clean energy solutions of tomorrow with American jobs today.

"Americans know we are in a race today for job creation, and that is a race with China to find out who is going to sell the products, and who is going to have the jobs in electric cars, in solar panels, in wind turbines, in efficiency, in electric charging stations, in new efficiencies to make our homes and businesses run more efficiently," Rep. Jay Inslee,

D-WA, said in a February 2011 House debate over clean air protections. "These are the jobs of the future," said Inslee. "If we're going to have these jobs of the future, we have to start moving off of this pollution."

THE CORE VALUES OF
THE AMERICAN PEOPLE

The House assault on our environment has put our future at risk in communities across the nation where a historic oil and gas drilling boom is playing out. It threatens American workers fighting to succeed in the global competition for the clean energy jobs of tomorrow. And it has contributed to the undermining of something worth far more than even all that: our faith in American democracy.

That faith rests on our bedrock belief that our voices will be heard and our intentions faithfully represented in a government that will help us, as a nation, to embrace the challenges, opportunities, and changes of our time. That takes principled leadership, certainly, and ideas born of vision and centered on workable solutions and the prospect of national gain. It also requires the ability to reconcile differences, broker compromise, and do the hard but essential work of finding common ground and building on it. The belief that the U.S. Congress is a place where that kind of work gets done has plunged to a historic low, as serious Americans on both sides of the political divide see the body as increasingly dysfunctional.

"How do we make rational choices in a Congress where leadership has broken down, lobbyists command so much power and where so many members have come to disdain compromise as betrayal?" conservative writer David Frum, who was a speechwriter for President George W. Bush, said in an October 2011 speech at Millikin University in Decatur, Illinois. "Remove the spirit of give and take from the system and the system breaks down—as it seems to be breaking down today."

With Congress enjoying the support of just 10 percent of the American public, it's clear that many are finding it harder all the time to regard that body as the effective seat of government by the people. That's more than a public embarrassment; it's a national crisis of confidence. There are many reasons for that crisis, and one is the widening gulf between the House assault on the American environment and the people's priorities and goals.

Time and time again last year, in a campaign that continued in the opening months of 2012, House Republicans voted in ways that conflicted directly with the powerful national consensus for protecting our environment and health and holding polluters accountable. Seven Americans in ten want the EPA to crack down on industrial greenhouse gas emissions and other pollution, an April 2011 CNN/Opinion Research Corp. poll found. By the same margin, Americans reject the false choice between a clean environment and good jobs, according to an October 2011 Public Policy Polling survey. Nearly three-fourths of the public (74 percent) supports increasing federal funding for research on wind, solar, and other sources of renewable power, a March 2011 poll by the Pew Research Center found. And even a solid majority (58 percent) of Republicans opposes House efforts to block the EPA from reducing air pollution from power plants, according to a summer 2011 poll by the GS Strategy Group and Hart Research Associates.

"Significant majorities support air and water quality laws," William Reilly, who served as EPA director under President George H. W. Bush, said in a Washington speech in November 2011. "This has been consistently true since the early 1970s, through the Arab oil embargo, high oil prices and recessions. As the late Bob Teeter, President George H. W. Bush's pollster, used to tell us, concern for the environment has entered the core values of the American people."

Reilly said he gave the speech in response to the campaign House Republicans waged against environmental safeguards, an effort conducted largely on the false claim that such protections were bad for jobs. "The widespread preoccupation with jobs and with economic growth has not made environmental protections less popular," said Reilly, a founding partner in Aqua International Partners, a private equity firm that invests in global water and renewable energy projects. "Research into concerns among CEOs of small businesses reveal that fully 80 percent do not see environmental regulations as having cost jobs or even figured in their concerns."

Republicans and their surrogates in the news media spent much of the year loudly asserting that the country must somehow choose between good jobs and a healthy environment. Despite the mainstream misinformation campaign, a solid American majority rejects that as a false choice.

In fact, it's rejected by a solid majority of Republicans: 58 percent of them oppose House efforts to block the EPA from reducing air pollution from power plants, despite GOP claims that it would hurt jobs. Those are the findings of a summer 2011 poll conducted jointly by the GS Strategy Group, a Republican public opinion research group, and Hart Research Associates, a Democratic pollster. In the same survey, 88 percent of Democrats opposed the move. The team conducted an online survey of 1,400 likely voters between August 31 and September 7, 2011.

The survey, commissioned by CERES, a Boston-based coalition of institutional investors and environmental advocates, found that 67 percent of voters, overall, support EPA efforts to reduce the soot and smog traveling across state lines from large coal-fired power plants. And 77 percent backed the new EPA standards to reduce the emissions of mercury and other pollution from such plants.

Similarly, 71 percent of Americans believe the EPA should enforce restrictions on greenhouse gas emissions and other pollution, according to an April 2011 CNN/Opinion Research Corp. poll of 824 adults nationwide. Just 28 percent supported the House effort to block the new EPA standards. House Republicans were out of step even with their own constituents. By a margin of 53–45, a majority percentage of Republicans said the EPA should be given the resources it needs to enforce the new rules. The margin was even wider among self-described conservatives, 56 percent of whom backed the new EPA rules, versus 44 percent who opposed them.

Perhaps no one watches these kinds of figures more closely than Lisa Jackson. A Tulane University graduate with a master's degree in chemical engineering from Princeton, she has devoted her career to standing up for a clean environment and public health, most recently by heading the EPA. As Jackson sees it, a fierce political battle is under way for the future of environmental protections and health. The public, she said, is on the right side of the contest.

"Today, there are two visions for the future of our environment and our economy," EPA Administrator Lisa Jackson said in a November 2011 speech to environmental law students and faculty at the University of California, Berkeley. "One says that we can rely on science, the law and innovation to protect our health and the environment and grow a sustainable, clean energy economy. The other vision says that moving forward requires rolling back standards for clean air and clean water. It says we have to increase protection for big polluters while reducing safeguards for the rest of us," she said. "After 40 years of progress, the American people still believe in the first vision."

"It is time to stop politicizing our air and water," said Jackson. "We are going to keep using science and the law to protect American families."

6

A RADICAL DEPARTURE

In June 1864, with the nation at war with itself, President Abraham Lincoln signed legislation setting aside a majestic expanse of California mountains, forests, and streams as the nation's first protected wilderness space. Six years later, President Ulysses S. Grant put his signature to the bill creating our first and most beloved national park, on land straddling Wyoming, Montana, and Idaho. And in 1903, President Theodore Roosevelt placed a Florida islet off limits to hunting and egg collecting, establishing the first American wildlife refuge. Together, these three presidents laid the foundation for what has become the largest and most comprehensive system of protected wilderness and wildlife habitat anywhere in the world.

In addition to their shared vision and commitment to protecting places that are now iconic in the American landscape—Yosemite, Yellowstone, and Pelican Island—Lincoln, Grant, and Roosevelt had something else in common. Each was a Republican, and each saw in the public preservation of nature a vital and indispensable role for government. Each understood, as Roosevelt put it in 1903, the "essential democracy" inherent in setting aside special places to ensure that future generations could experience the natural and unspoiled splendor of this vast and varied land. This was a part of our national inheritance that each of us could share, he said, in exchange for all of us, as a nation, "jealously safeguarding and preserving the scenery, the forests, and the creatures."

That same year, ordering a mandate of conscience with the stroke of a pen, Roosevelt designated tiny Pelican Island, at the mouth of Florida's Indian River, the country's first federal bird preserve. Over the next six years, he created five more, ranging from the Gulf of Mexico to the Alaskan Yukon.

An avid outdoorsman and inveterate conservationist, Roosevelt had witnessed, in his lifetime, the near extermination of bison across the Great Plains, jaguars along the Rio Grande, and egrets, herons, and spoonbills from the marshy lagoons of Florida. As he placed American lands beyond the reach of hunters, miners, furriers, and egg collectors, and commissioned wardens to defend special places from poachers, Roosevelt drew the ire and opposition of corporate interests and their Washington lobbyists, who sought to turn back environmental progress to protect their profits.

Roosevelt's opponents, though, were no match for the determined Rough Rider. Hardly one to cower or cater to the industrial bullies of his day, Roosevelt fought back, making "the scrawl of his signature, a conservationist weapon," as his biographer, Douglas Brinkley, wrote.

In the final year of his second term in office, Roosevelt brought state governors, members of Congress, Supreme Court justices, and others to a White House environmental summit, where he tied the need for national conservation to the cherished history of united efforts and common action that bore the nation's Constitution and, indeed, the Republic itself.

"The wise use of all of our natural resources, which are our national resources as well, is the great material question of today," Roosevelt told the group, "and the threat of imminent exhaustion of some of them, due to reckless and wasteful use, once more calls for common effort, common action."

Through a series of decisions to take the kind of common action Roosevelt both called for and began, Americans have set aside more than 635 million acres of national parks, forests, refuge areas, waterways, and federally managed lands for posterity. Together, those lands make up about one fourth of the United States, an area roughly the size of the land President Thomas Jefferson bought from France when he made the Louisiana Purchase.

It's hard to imagine how those national treasures might have been preserved, and frightening to consider the alternative, had the first Republican president of the twentieth century not stood up for the American environment.

"In a fundamental way, Roosevelt was a conservation visionary, aware of the pitfalls of hyper-industrialization, fearful that speed-logging, blast-rock mining, overgrazing, reckless hunting, oil drilling, population growth, and all types of pollution would leave the planet in biological peril," Brinkley wrote in his masterful 2009 book *The Wilderness Warrior: Theodore Roosevelt and the Crusade for America.* "As forces of globalization run amok, Roosevelt's stout resoluteness to protect our environment is a strong reminder of our national wilderness heritage, as well as an increasingly urgent call to arms."

POLLUTERS MUST PAY

That call was answered, to a greater or lesser degree, by other Republican presidents extending from the middle of the twentieth century nearly to its end.

It was Republican President Dwight Eisenhower who established the Arctic National Wildlife Refuge in 1960, setting aside unique Alaskan wilderness areas that are home to caribou, snow geese, Pacific herring, and grizzly bears. Even amid the preoccupations and existential threats he confronted in the early years of the Cold War, Eisenhower warned against the same kind of waste and recklessness that troubled Roosevelt decades before.

"As we peer into society's future, we—you and I, and our government—must avoid the impulse to live only for today, plundering, for our own ease and convenience, the precious resources of tomorrow," Eisenhower said in his 1961 farewell address to the nation. "We cannot mortgage the material assets of our grandchildren without asking the loss also of their political and spiritual heritage."

President Ronald Reagan built on the Eisenhower legacy, expanding the Arctic National Wildlife Refuge, now 19.6 million acres of protected watershed and habitat. Reagan also tried, unsuccessfully, to get Congress to approve oil and gas drilling in the refuge. Congress pushed back, reminding Reagan that the Arctic National Wildlife Refuge was part of the larger natural inheritance bequeathed to future generations by American leaders reaching back to Lincoln. Reagan had an antiregulatory zeal that sometimes led to excesses that put our environment and health at risk. He insisted, though, that corporate interests strike a balance with the need to safeguard our natural resources. And he recognized that doing so was not a partisan objective, but, rather, a common goal that was good for the country.

"If we've learned any lessons during the past few decades, perhaps the most important is that preservation of our environment is not a partisan challenge; it's common sense," Reagan said during a 1984 visit to Washington's Theodore Roosevelt Island, an eighty-eight-acre memorial in the Potomac River. "Our physical health, our social happiness, and our economic well-being will be sustained only by all of us working in partnership as thoughtful, effective stewards of our natural resources."

Like Reagan, his Republican successor, President George H. W. Bush, pushed unsuccessfully to allow oil drilling at the Arctic National Wildlife Refuge. Environmentalists opposed the Bush administration over that, as well as on biodiversity policies, wetlands protections, and other issues. Bush, though, overcame sharp divisions among Democrats and Republicans, and even his own cabinet, to pass historic legislation that strengthened the Clean Air Act in ways that dramatically improved the nation's air quality.

"I want to broaden the consensus for a clean environment," Bush said in February 1989, less than three weeks into his presidency. With Democrats holding majorities in the House and Senate, Bush said "Our great common desire is a better life for all Americans. And I believe that economic growth and a clean environment are both part of what all Americans understand a better life to mean."

Four months later, with echoes of Roosevelt's grand conservation summitry, Bush summoned state governors, congressional leaders from both political parties, corporate executives, environmentalists, and others to the White House, where he issued an emphatic appeal for the varied interests to work together for cleaner air.

"I reject the notion that sound ecology and a strong economy are mutually exclusive," Bush declared in remarks to the assembled group in the ornate East Room. "Every American expects and deserves to breathe clean air, and as president, it is my mission to guarantee it—for this generation and for the generations to come."

It took patience, compromise, and hard work, but Bush prevailed, returning to the same White House room sixteen months later to sign the 1990 Clean Air Act amendments.

"We have succeeded today because of a common sense of global stewardship, a sense that it is the Earth that endures and that all of us are simply holding a sacred trust left for future generations," Bush said to a group that included many of the people who'd been in the East Room when he laid out his vision the year before. "American heritage is precious," he said. "We will not turn our backs or look the other way. That means polluters must pay."

WHAT WE LEAVE TO OUR CHILDREN

The Bush amendments to the Clean Air Act led to EPA actions that dramatically reduced the air pollution that causes acid rain. The amendments also called for new EPA standards to reduce urban smog and ozone, as well as mercury and other toxic chemicals, the very provisions House Republicans voted to block in 2011.

In their reckless assault on the safeguards we all rely on to protect our environment and health, in fact, the new House majority turned its back on more than a century of the GOP's own history, a Republican legacy of conservation that extends back to Teddy Roosevelt and even to Lincoln. The votes betrayed the promise of environmental stewardship Republican presidents have made to successive generations of Americans. And they cut against the grain of some of the most fundamental tenets of conservative thought, the political and philosophical cornerstones, many Republicans assert, upon which the party stands.

"What is a conservative, after all, but one who conserves, one who is committed to protecting and holding close the things by which we live," Reagan asked during dedication ceremonies for the National Geographic Society's Washington, D.C., headquarters building in June 1984. "Modern conservatives in America want to protect and preserve the values and traditions by which the nation has flourished for more than two centuries," Reagan said. "And we want to protect and conserve the land on which we live—our countryside, our rivers and mountains, our plains and meadows and forests. This is our patrimony. This is what we leave to our children. And our great moral responsibility is to leave it to them either as we found it or better than we found it."

Like others of his era, Reagan's political philosophy was informed, in large part, by the writings of Russell Kirk, a historian and critic widely regarded as the father of modern conservatism. Reagan called Kirk "a great conservative intellect and scholar" and awarded him the Presidential Citizens Medal for his life's work. Kirk's 1953 political opus, *The Conservative Mind*, is a seminal overview that has guided generations of Republican thought.

Writing of the same age that prompted Eisenhower to issue his warnings against the plunder of industry at the expense of the nation's future, Kirk wrote that conservatives bore a special obligation to future generations.

"The noun 'conservative' signifies guardian or defender, the conservator," Kirk wrote in his 1953 classic. And it was up to conservatives, he wrote, to insist upon responsible environmental stewardship.

"Men's appetites are voracious and sanguinary," Kirk wrote. "If men are discharged of reverence for ancient usage, they will treat this world, almost certainly, as if it were their private property, to be consumed for their sensual gratification; and thus they will destroy in their lust for enjoyment the property of future generations, of their own contemporaries, and indeed their very own capital."

Reaching back through decades of early conservative thought, Kirk lays out an intellectual and moral argument for environmental protection that today's environmental movement would do well to revisit. Kirk warns against a vision of environmental devastation that eerily mirrors much of what the House majority voted in 2011 to create.

"The modern spectacle of vanished forests and eroded lands, wasted petroleum and ruthless mining, national debts recklessly increased until they are repudiated, and continual revision of positive law, is evidence of what an age without veneration does to itself and its successors," Kirk warned six decades ago.

The roots of conservative thought, of course, run far deeper than that, originating, scholars contend, in the writings of Edmund Burke, the eighteenth-century Irish political philosopher and parliamentarian.

Writing at the dawn of the industrial age, Burke warned against the abuse of resources by "temporary possessors" who "commit waste on the inheritance" and "leave to those who come after them a ruin instead of a habitation." By breaking faith with future generations, he

wrote, national bonds of continuity would be severed. "No one generation could link with another. Men would become little better than the
flies of a summer."

The buzz of impending decay can faintly be heard in Kirk's own
summation of how conservative ideals were hijacked in the years following World War I, when, in Kirk's words, "practical conservatism
degenerated into mere laudation of 'private enterprise,' economic policy
almost wholly surrendered to special interests." Either Kirk had a gift
for seeing the future or history is tragically repeating itself. Either way,
warns Kirk, "such a nation was inviting the catastrophes which compel
society to re-examine first principles."

The nation's founders relied on few first principles more than those
of the personal thrift and self-reliance required of an independent people. Like so many other pillars of conservative teaching, those ideals have
been cast aside in the GOP flight from its environmental moorings, inviting future catastrophe, to be sure. In 2011, the party roared headlong
through a year of slashing support for programs aimed at making our
homes and businesses more efficient or developing the renewable power
that can reduce our costly and dangerous dependence on foreign oil and
generate American prosperity without undue environmental harm.

"Any restraint on material appetites, even efficiency measures that
make a dollar go further, is the enemy of a political ideology that places
a premium on material gain and immediate gratification," David Jenkins,
vice president for government and political affairs with Republicans for
Environmental Protection, a nonprofit Washington advocacy group,
wrote in a December 2011 blog. "This is not conservatism. There is
nothing conservative about waste and gluttony."

There is nothing conservative, either, about ignoring medical
warnings and putting polluters first at the expense of the public, allowing
smokestack industries and other special interests to poison our air, pollute our water, and put our health at risk for the sake of corporate profits.

"Normally, the country can count on conservatives to deal in facts.
We base policies on science, not sentiment, we insist on people being
accountable for their actions, and we maintain that markets, not man-
dates, are the path to prosperity," former Rep. Bob Inglis, R–SC, wrote
on the Bloomberg news web site in October 2011. "When it comes
to energy and climate, these are not normal times. We're following

sentiment, not science, we're turning a blind eye to accountability and we're failing to use the power of markets."

At its core, in fact, the entire body of environmental law that has guided the nation for four decades represents some of "the oldest and best sense" of traditional conservatism, economists Frank Ackerman and Lisa Heinzerling wrote in their 2004 book, *Priceless: On Knowing the Price of Everything and the Value of Nothing*. These laws, the authors wrote, help to restore "values like humility, fairness, and a sense of moral urgency to a central place in our relationships with one another and with the environment."

It is these very principles and values that have been placed in jeopardy by the GOP pivot from its own history and philosophical underpinnings. How did the House Republicans move so quickly from their own party's environmental legacy and so far from the traditions of modern conservatism? The answer, according to political analysts, scholars, and Republicans themselves, is that much of the party has been captured by a virulent combination of tea party anger, corporate cash, and the fears of the ultra right wing, at a time when the GOP's two-step program for change—reduced public investment and less public oversight of corporate polluters—would do the struggling economy more harm than good.

"Republicans have a problem," Bruce Bartlett, a former economic adviser to President Ronald Reagan, wrote in an October 4 column for *The New York Times* web site. "People are increasingly concerned about unemployment, but Republicans have nothing to offer them."

Federal spending cuts will force government layoffs, raising joblessness, and dampening the consumer demand needed to fuel economic recovery. "Republicans favor tax cuts for the wealthy and corporations, but these had no stimulative effect during the George W. Bush administration and there is no reason to believe that more of them will have any today," Bartlett wrote, expressing sentiments echoed by other Republicans as well.

"In the face of evidence of dwindling upward mobility and long-stagnating middle-class wages, my party's economic ideas sometimes seem to have shrunk to just one: more tax cuts for the very highest earners," conservative author David Frum, who served as a speechwriter to former President George W. Bush, wrote in *New York* magazine in November 2011. "When I entered Republican politics, during an earlier period of malaise, in the late seventies and early eighties, the movement got most of the big questions—crime, inflation, the Cold War—right. This time, the party is getting the big questions disastrously wrong."

Absent concrete proposals with a track record of success, House Republicans spent 2011 peddling the myth that job growth can be sparked by dismantling public safeguards. Kirk leaves little doubt as to how he would reply to the Republican broadside against "job-killing regulations" and similar bumper-sticker replies to serious national ills.

"Any informed conservative is reluctant to condense profound and intricate intellectual systems to a few pretentious phrases; he prefers to leave that technique to the enthusiasm of radicals," wrote Kirk. "Conservatism is not a fixed and immutable body of dogmata."

Or, at least, it didn't used to be. The recent House record on our environment and health, though, is an open window into just how badly the party has lost its way.

"An understanding of, and appreciation of, the environment has been part of the ethos of the Republican Party from its very founding," said former Gov. Christine Todd Whitman, a Republican who served as administrator of the Environmental Protection Agency under President George W. Bush.

"We basically started the whole thing," said Whitman. "The first president to set aside public lands was Abraham Lincoln. Richard Nixon was the one who established the Environmental Protection Agency. Reagan continued that. George W. Bush continued it. Those were all Republican presidents working with a Democratically controlled Congress. That's when people understood that there are some issues that go beyond partisan politics."

Throughout 2001 and in the early months of 2012, House Republicans largely abandoned that legacy, putting hard-won historical gains at risk.

"It is a huge shift, one that embarrasses many former Republican officials who were strong environmentalists," said Thomas Mann, a congressional scholar with the Brookings Institution, a nonpartisan but generally progressive Washington think tank. Mann addresses the party's sharp departure from its environmental roots as part of a larger change in a forthcoming book he has authored with Norman Ornstein, a congressional scholar with the American Enterprise Institute, a nonpartisan but conservative-leaning Washington think tank.

"One of our two major parties, the Republicans, has become an insurgent outlier—ideologically extreme, contemptuous of the inherited social and economic policy regime, scornful of compromise, unpersuaded by conventional understanding of facts, evidence, and science, and dismissive of the legitimacy of its political opposition," Mann and Ornstein, two of the most respected political analysts in Washington, wrote in their 2012 book *It's Even Worse Thank It Looks: America's Dysfunctional Politics*. "When one party moves this far from the center of American politics, it is extremely difficult to enact policies responsive to our most pressing challenges."

The Republican Party has strayed far from its history as a big tent that could accommodate an array of centrists, moderates, and even progressives along a wide spectrum of conservative thought. Instead, it has narrowed its focus. Centrists and moderates have been marginalized. Progressives have been eliminated.

"The GOP has, for all intents and purposes, become a uniformly ideological party unlike any that has ever existed in American history," wrote Geoffrey Kabaservice, a former assistant professor of history at Yale University. "It has also become a party that has cut itself off from its own history, and indeed has become antagonistic to most of its own heritage," Kabaservice wrote in his 2012 book *Rule and Ruin: The Downfall of Moderation and the Destruction of the Republican Party, from Eisenhower to the Tea Party*. "In today's Republican Party, moderates—and indeed entire regions of the country where moderates predominate—are essentially unrepresented."

In their place are members largely marching in lockstep along unyielding lines enforced by litmus tests meant to ensure ideological purity regarding a growing list of issues ranging from tax cuts (need more), to climate change (not happening), and new clean air standards (nope).

Of the 242 Republicans in the House, for example, 236 have signed a pledge promising that they will not raise tax rates or reduce tax deductions or credits for individuals or businesses. The Speaker of the House, John Boehner of Ohio, has taken the pledge; so has the House Majority Leader, Eric Cantor of Virginia. Of the 192 House Democrats,

2 have signed. The pledge is the brainchild of Grover Norquist, founder of the conservative advocacy group, Americans for Tax Reform, and author of the 2008 book *Leave Us Alone: Getting the Government's Hands Off Our Money, Our Guns, Our Lives.*

Here is where the spirit of compromise withers and dies, and the will to reconcile honest political differences gets ground to powder. The bipartisan Simpson-Bowles debt reduction panel—formally known as the National Commission on Fiscal Responsibility and Reform—stated flat out in December 2010 that the only way to balance our federal budget and avert fiscal disaster is to cut spending and raise taxes. It's simple math.

"America cannot be great if we go broke," the commission concluded. "Everything must be on the table."

How, exactly, can Congress address this issue when the House majority has promised Grover Norquist that revenue gains are off the table? How does the country benefit when one party demonstrates its willingness to allow the United States government to default on its debt in order to underscore its intransigence on that point, as the House majority did last summer? Who wins when the result is a downgrade of U.S. credit worthiness and troubling questions about the future of the U.S. dollar as the currency of global trade?

In much the same light, the nation is being asked to bear a withering ideological attack on the foundational environmental safeguards put in place by generations of leaders from both parties, and for much the same reason: the Republican center has simply collapsed, to the great detriment of our political institutions and the possibility of effective governance in times of challenge.

"If, as many observers believe, the American political system proves unable to make necessary reforms to meet the long-term challenges posed by energy dependence, environmental degradation, Social Security's shaky economic foundation, and the rising tide of government deficits and pension liabilities, the absence of the moderate Republicans may be the single greatest explanatory factor," Kabaservice writes. "If American politics can be compared to an ecosystem, then the disappearance of the moderate Republicans represents a catastrophic loss of species diversity."

7

CORPORATE CLOUT
AND TEA PARTY RAGE

The weeding out of Republican moderates has been the work of a generation, fraught with fits and starts running from Barry Goldwater's nomination as the GOP presidential candidate in 1964—he was trounced by Lyndon Johnson—through the two-term Reagan presidency and the administration of President George W. Bush and Vice President Dick Cheney. Among House Republicans, though, the killing off of the species reached a tipping point with the 2009 rise of the tea party, a national political movement of an estimated 45 million Americans aided and abetted by conservative news media and some of the wealthiest corporate polluters in the country.

Loosely led by some 200,000 activists in 1,000 organizations in all fifty states, tea party supporters generally describe themselves in polls as very conservative. They self-define the term as someone who supports low taxes, limited government, and the kind of free-market vision roughly summed up in the title to Grover Norquist's book: *Leave Us Alone*—except when it comes to providing roads and airports, military defense, pharmaceuticals research, retirement and medical benefits, and the like and doling out public subsidies to oil and gas companies, nuclear power plants, and other favored industries. As a group, tea party supporters tend to rail out against government corruption, while vesting somewhat more faith in corporations, disdaining federal regulation of the financial services industry even in the wake of the 2008 Wall Street collapse that triggered the Great Recession.

Those are among the findings of Harvard University government and sociology professor Theda Skocpol, a past president of the American Political Science Association. Working with Harvard PhD candidate

Vanessa Williamson, she has studied the tea party and its impact on Republicans since the movement's 2009 beginnings. The two scholars sum up their conclusions in the 2012 book *The Tea Party and the Remaking of Republican Conservatism*, which lays out the movement's rise to national prominence on the wings of heartland anger, corporate greed, and the fear and anxiety fed by Fox News and other conservative media that form what the authors call the "right-wing noise and echo machine" that aims to keep followers perpetually on edge.

"Grassroots activists, roving billionaire advocates, and right-wing media purveyors—these three forces together create the tea party and give it the ongoing clout to buffet and redirect the Republican Party and influence broader debates in American democracy," Skocpol and Williamson wrote. "Democrats have no hope of attracting tea party support, no matter how hard they tack toward the right—especially not while Barack Obama, virtually the Devil incarnate for Tea Partiers, remains in the White House."

In 2009, Americans got an ugly glimpse of how deep the group's hatred toward Obama can run, when tea party Republican Joe Wilson of South Carolina disgraced his constituents and embarrassed his colleagues by bellowing out "You lie" to the president of the United States as Obama delivered a speech on health care reforms before a joint session of Congress.

Consigned to the political wilderness in the wake of the 2008 elections, which left Democrats in control of the White House and both houses of Congress, Republicans found common cause with tea party supporters in the lead-up to the 2010 midterm elections, seeing in the rise of this grassroots prairie fire their pathway back to power. The House Tea Party Caucus, headed by Rep. Michelle Bachmann, R-MN, lists sixty members, all Republicans, including seventeen freshmen first elected in 2010 and forty-three representatives who won reelection that year.

House Majority Leader Eric Cantor, R-VA, is not a formal member of the caucus, but he's been a big supporter of the movement and its causes. Like many members of Congress, Cantor runs a leadership political action committee, or PAC, which enables him to collect money he can then dole out to help others become elected. During the 2010 elections, Cantor's Every Republican Is Crucial (ERIC) PAC, was the largest such leadership PAC in the country, gathering $1.7 million—more even than the $1.3 million raised by House Speaker John Boehner's Freedom Project PAC. Among the top ten contributors to Cantor's leadership PAC are Alpha Natural Resources, one of the nation's largest coal companies; the Altria Group, the largest cigarette maker in the world; and global investment banks like Goldman Sachs, Morgan Stanley, and Credit Suisse (no wonder Cantor used the word "mobs" to describe the Occupy Wall Street protesters).

Cantor's leadership PAC was a big tea party supporter, contributing a total of $330,600—or just under $8,000 each on average—to forty two of the sixty tea party Republicans who won election to the House, according to the Center for Responsive Politics. By November 2011, Cantor had already contributed more than $100,000 to tea party candidates for the 2012 elections.

While many tea party supporters describe themselves as political independents, they hew, as a group, well to the right of the Republican mainstream. Of the 9 percent of the public that self-identifies as "staunch conservatives," 72 percent say they agree with the tea party, compared with just 32 percent of what some analysts call "Main Street" Republicans, a May 2011 poll by the Pew Research Center found. Those differences show up sharply on economic questions, according to extensive research done by Emily Ekins, a graduate student at the University of California, Los Angeles. Among tea party Republicans, 80 percent are opposed to raising taxes on people who make more than $250,000 a year, compared to 56 percent opposition among Republicans who are not tea party supporters. And when asked whether the federal government should spend money to create jobs or focus on cutting government spending, 76 percent of tea party Republicans favored spending cuts compared to 47 percent of other Republicans.

On support for renewable power, tea party supporters are, again, well to the right of Republicans generally.

Among the general public, 63 percent say that developing wind, solar, and other forms of alternative energy should take priority over expanding the use of oil, coal, and natural gas, the May 2011 Pew poll discovered. Among Main Street Republicans, the figure is 66 percent—higher than among the public at large. Among the staunch conservatives that widely support the tea party, though, just 15 percent support renewable power over fossil fuels.

Republican voters are deeply split over environmental protections as well, and the divide largely reflects the difference between tea party backers and Main Street Republicans.

Among tea party Republicans, 68 percent favor cuts in environmental protections and just 9 percent support stronger safeguards, according to a February 2011 Pew poll. Among Republicans who said they are not tea party backers, just 31 percent favored such cuts; 23 percent said environmental protections should be increased.

While Americans generally get a media mosaic of tea party backers as heartland members of the middle class, their elected representatives are anything but that.

"The members of the House Tea Party Caucus are especially wealthy," the Center for Responsive Politics wrote in a 2011 report. "The median average net worth of a member of the House Tea Party Caucus was $1.8 million in 2010," the center's analysis found. That's more than double the average for House members generally, who have a median average net worth of $755,000.

The tea party crowd's anti-government fervor fits neatly with the corporate agenda of companies that profit most when others bear the costs of their pollution, or when our factories and cars burn more of the fossil fuels that poison our air with toxic chemicals and industrial carbon, soot, and smog.

The oil and gas industry has long been among the most powerful influence peddlers in Washington. Since 1990, individuals and PACs associated with the industry have ponied up $239 million in campaign contributions. Most has gone to Republicans who support industry goals like limiting environmental protections, blocking measures to reduce climate change, and allowing drilling in the Alaska National Wildlife Refuge. Over just the past five years, the industry has spent $686.6 million pressing its priorities in Washington alone, deploying an army of nearly 800 lobbyists to twist arms, curry favor, and cut off political opponents at the knees.

No one, it seems, is immune to the bullying and threats of Big Oil.

The industry's top lobbyist warned in January 2012 that Obama would face "huge political consequences" unless he approves the Keystone XL tar sands pipeline the oil companies want to run from Canada to the Gulf of Mexico. Jack Gerard, president of the American

Petroleum Institute, the industry trade association, said rejecting the pipeline would be a "huge mistake" for Obama. "Clearly the Keystone XL pipeline is in the national interest" and should be approved, Gerard said in a speech at an API meeting. "A determination to decide anything less than that, I believe, will have huge political consequences."

The oil and gas industry got out early in support of tea party candidates. By July 2010, industry employees and associates had donated an average of more than $25,000 each to tea party congressional candidates, a Center for Responsive Politics analysis found.

The tea party movement has continued to receive critical support from wealthy industrial chieftains, whose twin goals of defeating Obama in 2012 and eviscerating public oversights to enhance their corporate profits fit like a set of political brass knuckles on the angry hands of the tea party crowd. The tea party movement's anti-regulatory, pro-business bias has been exploited, if not hijacked wholesale, by some of the biggest polluters in the country, which spend heavily to combat safeguards needed to promote a clean environment and public health.

Two of the movement's biggest financial supporters are David and Charles Koch, petrochemical and paper industrialists with a combined worth Forbes magazine estimates at some $50 billion. Tea party animosity toward Obama is a comfortable fit for these two. In May 2011, David Koch told a New York magazine reporter that "Obama's a hardcore socialist . . . . He's scary to me." In February 2012, the Koch brothers vowed to raise $100 million to defeat Obama.

Together, the Koch brothers own a majority interest in Koch Industries, the second-largest privately held company in the country, with 2011 revenues estimated at $100 billion. Based in Wichita, Kansas, the company owns oil refineries in Alaska, Texas, and Minnesota, as well as a large maker of carpets, fibers, and insulation and the Georgia-Pacific pulp, paper, and building products company. Koch Industries is the tenth biggest polluter in the nation, according to a 2010 study by the University of Massachusetts' Political Economy Research Institute, based on EPA emissions data.

Koch Industries is hardly a household name. It casts a long shadow, though. In Washington, the company has spent $54 million over just the past five years lobbying against policies like air quality safeguards, clean energy legislation, and efforts to reduce the industrial carbon pollution that is warming the planet. In addition, people or organizations associated with Koch Industries contributed $2.2 million to congressional candidates who backed their industry-driven agenda in the 2010 midterm elections. Most of the money—93 percent—went to Republicans, according to the Center for Responsive Politics.

The money isn't sprinkled around at random. During the 2010 midterm elections, Koch employees and associates contributed a total of $217,900 to thirty-seven of the tea party Republicans, freshmen and incumbents, who were elected to Congress. That averages out to just under $6,000 per candidate, although the actual contributions ranged in size from $1,000 to Tom McClintock of California to $12,650 to Eric Cantor, the House Majority Leader.

Koch employees and associates contributed a total of $279,500 to the campaign coffers of twenty two of the thirty-one Republicans on the House Energy and Commerce Committee, which has broad jurisdiction over much of the environmental legislation that impacts Koch businesses. The committee's chairman, Fred Upton, R-MI, received $12,000. Of the twelve new Republicans on the panel, nine signed a pledge distributed by a Koch-founded advocacy group to oppose the Obama administration's effort to reduce the greenhouse gases that are warming our planet, *The Los Angeles Times* reported in February 2011. The Kochs are well underway with an assertive campaign to keep tea party freshmen in Congress, having made sizable contributions already—$7,000 to Tim Walberg of Michigan, $5,000 to Steven Palazzo of Mississippi, $6,000 to Tim Huelskamp of Kansas, and $4,500 to Blake Farenthold of Texas, to name a few—to their 2012 campaigns.

In January 2011, as GOP members were preparing to assume the majority role in the new Congress, David Koch praised the tea party movement and the role Americans for Prosperity had played in its ascent to national prominence.

"There are some extremists there, but the rank and file are just normal people like us," Koch told Lee Fang, a blogger with the left-leaning Think Progress blog. "I admire them," Koch said of the tea party movement. "It's probably the best grassroots uprising since 1776, in my opinion."

With the rise of the tea party, the Koch brothers have aligned themselves and their political largesse with a grassroots following, in a wedding of convenience that links the Koch brothers' anti-regulatory agenda with a national movement that can bring tens of millions of voters to the polls.

In addition to direct contributions, the Koch empire brings campaign assistance—organizing rallies, town hall meetings, phone banks, transportation, door-to-door canvassing, advocacy training, speakers and so on—either in support of favored candidates or in opposition to others, through Americans for Prosperity. A powerful conservative PAC co-founded by David Koch, the organization advocates for cuts in federal taxes and against environmental safeguards and other regulations. It also initiated the greenhouse gas pledge that so many members of the House Energy and Commerce Committee signed. Tagging itself "America's premier grassroots organization," the group lists 1.9 million activists in fifty states.

During the 2010 midterm elections, Americans for Prosperity provided $40 million worth of support for candidates in more than 100 congressional races across the country, according to *The Los Angeles Times*. The group hosted more than 500 bus rallies and town hall meetings, advocating the evisceration of environmental safeguards with themes like "Regulation Reality Tour," calling for even deeper tax cuts and hosting a "Cost of Hot Air Tour" to build opposition against EPA limits on the industrial carbon pollution that is driving global climate change.

"Congress needs to step in and stop the EPA, which is an out-of-control rogue agency," the Americans for Prosperity vice president for policy, Phil Kerpen, wrote in an August 2011 blog for the *National Journal*, going on to decry what he called the EPA's "astonishingly anti-growth agenda."

In a February 2012 post on its web site, the group gave a succinct view of Obama's presidency: "more taxes, more government, and job killing regulations," a decent summary, as well, of all Americans for Prosperity opposed.

"The Koch brothers do not so much believe in limited government as in almost no government at all," wrote Skocpol and Williamson. "The tea party eruption in early 2009 was just what the doctor ordered for far-right ideological billionaires like the Kochs, and others of their ideological ilk roving just beyond the edge of the GOP establishment."

The Koch brothers counter that such criticism is unfair. Writing on their behalf in the *Wall Street Journal* in February 2012, Koch attorney Theodore Olson, a respected Washington lawyer and former U.S. Solicitor General, contends that the petrochemical magnates have become "an attractive political punching bag" for their left-wing opponents, from the White House on down.

"What Messrs. Koch do, in fact, is manage businesses that provide employment to more than 50,000 people in North America in legitimate, productive industries," Olson wrote. "Their biggest offense, apparently, is that they also contribute generously to nonprofit organizations that promote personal liberty and free enterprise, and some of those organizations oppose policies advocated by the president."

Business executives like the Kochs are entitled to speak up for their interests. They have that right. But something is terribly wrong when corporate and private wealth can be used to drown out the voices of individual voters, distort the essential democratic processes of elections and legislation, and drive elected representatives to focus on the priorities of the biggest corporate donors at the expense of the public interest.

Politicians resent the charge that their vote can be bought. But does anyone believe corporations like Koch Industries spend millions of dollars bankrolling political campaigns because they happen to like the candidates?

"Our Congress is politically bankrupt," Harvard law professor Lawrence Lessig concludes in his 2011 book *Republic, Lost: How Money Corrupts Congress—and a Plan to Stop It.* "Our government doesn't track the will of the people, whether on the left or the right. Instead, the government tracks a different interest, one not directly affected by votes or voters. Democracy, on this account, seems a show or a ruse; power rests elsewhere," wrote Lessig. "When democracy seems a charade," he wrote, "we lose faith in its process."

In April 2009, veteran Rep. Fred Upton, R-MI, posted a message on his web site, noting that "Climate change is a serious problem that necessitates serious solutions. Everything must be on the table—particularly renewable sources of energy like wind and solar, nuclear power and clean coal technologies."

It was hardly a radical statement, particularly for Upton, a moderate Republican who had a good record on environmental issues. The year before, the League of Conservation Voters found that he'd voted on the pro-environment side of issues 54 percent of the time, supporting tax credits for clean energy, public transportation grants, green building standards, and other forward-looking measures.

By December 2010, though, a month after winning reelection with the help of $290,700 in campaign contributions from the electric utilities and oil and gas industries, Upton had changed his mind on climate. After tea party Republicans threatened to block his ultimately successful bid to become chairman of the House Energy and Commerce Committee, Upton teamed up with Tim Phillips to write an op-ed that appeared in the *Wall Street Journal*, in which the authors wrote "We are not convinced" that carbon is a problem in need of regulation. Phillips is the president of Americans for Prosperity. Suddenly, with help from his backers at Koch, Upton had come to realize that EPA rules to reduce carbon emissions were no longer part of the "serious solutions" needed to combat climate change, but rather, "an unconstitutional power grab that will kill millions of jobs," as he wrote in the op-ed. Why, Upton fumed, if the EPA is allowed to reduce carbon pollution from refineries, paper mills, and other smokestack industries like those the Koch brothers own, "churches and perhaps even single-family homes" could be next.

This is exactly the kind of fear-mongering that goes down so well at tea party rallies and on conservative radio and television shows, and it was no accident. Because there was more to Upton's change of climate heart, it turns out, than campaign contributions. In the spring of 2010, while serving his twelfth term in Congress, Upton had a scare, when a tea party candidate challenged his seat in a GOP primary contest. Upton survived the challenge, winning 57 percent of the primary vote. That's not exactly a comfortable margin for a long-time incumbent, and Upton heavily outspent his opponent to win.

Others in his party weren't so lucky.

Former Rep. Bob Inglis, R-SC, was trounced in a primary challenge by Spartanburg County solicitor Trey Gowdy, who won the backing of his district's tea party crowd and criticized Inglis for, among other things, opposing oil drilling in Alaska's Arctic National Wildlife Refuge. In twelve years in Congress, Inglis was among the most conservative members of the House. The American Conservative Union gave him a lifetime voting score of 93.5 percent. He was endorsed by the

National Rifle Association and National Right to Life. Inglis, though, wasn't conservative enough for the tea party wing of his constituency. Some were enraged when he challenged voters in town hall meetings who questioned Obama's citizenship or patriotism. Others jeered when he urged them to turn off popular Fox News pundits he said were trafficking in falsehood and fear.

"To encourage that kind of fear is just the lowest form of political leadership. It's not leadership. It's demagoguery," Inglis told the Associated Press in July 2010, after he'd lost to Gowdy. "What it takes to lead is to say, 'You know, that's just not right.'"

Gowdy went on to easily win his district congressional seat in the 2010 elections, with 63 percent of the vote. As is the case in many congressional districts across the country, Gowdy's has been mapped out to favor Republicans, just as many other districts nationwide are drawn so as to favor Democrats. The result, in many cases, is that the districts aren't competitive between parties. That means the primary races are where the contest gets decided. And primaries are the domain of the relatively small percentage of the party's base that generally determines the outcome.

As a result, the fear for many Republicans, at least in 2010, was that they would be challenged by someone from the far right wing, who could galvanize the conservative base. That, analysts say, helped to push the whole party to the right, with Inglis serving as an example of what might happen to those who refused to shift to the right, and Upton an example of how things turned out for those who did. Many Republicans who in the past might have tried to strike a different kind of balance in their approach to environmental legislation got the message that they would become tea party targets if they took a more supportive approach. Some, in essence, were running scared from the kind of "demagoguery" that sidelined Inglis.

The tea party crowd loudly criticizes the Washington culture and congressional subservience to special interests. Once in office, however, the tea party House members proved surprisingly malleable. During their first nine months in office, fifteen tea party freshmen hauled in $3.5 million in donations from almost 700 different political action committees, a joint analysis by the Center for Responsive Politics and the Center for Public Integrity found. The five largest donors were two defense contractors—Honeywell and Lockheed Martin—the American Bankers Association, the National Association of Realtors, and Koch Industries.

As newcomers see piles of campaign cash as the key to staying in office "they go to the people and interests who are more than happy to give it—those who want something from Congress," said Mary Boyle, spokeswoman for Common Cause, a nonprofit organization that monitors government influence peddling in Washington. That must change, Boyle said in an article posted on the Center for Public Integrity web site, "so that lawmakers don't take office owing favors to their biggest campaign donors."

EPILOGUE

A BETTER LAND

It isn't often that the president of the United States takes time out to visit a federal agency to buck up the spirits of the rank and file. In January 2012, though, President Obama did just that. He went to the headquarters of the Environmental Protection Agency, a few blocks from the White House, to remind Administrator Lisa Jackson and those who work for her of the "vital mission" they serve.

"Our environment is safer because of you," Obama told them. "Our country is stronger because of you. Our future is brighter because of you. And I want you to know that you've got a president who is grateful for your work and will stand with you every inch of the way as you carry out your mission to make sure that we've got a cleaner world."

Behind the cheers and applause that followed stood an environmental corps that badly needed the rhetorical balm. For an entire year, they had endured the unrelenting criticism and political cheap shots of a House majority bent on undermining national support for the EPA and the essential public oversight function it serves.

Presidential speeches, though, are never just words. In speaking, a president acts. Obama was drawing a line in the sand for every American to see. Using the EPA headquarters as his stage, Obama made clear that he would not be cowed by the political assault on the American environment, but would stand up instead for the foundational safeguards we all depend on to protect our environment and health.

Standing on the shoulders of presidents from both political parties who have served before him, Obama pledged to keep faith with

American generations to come. Not only would he work to defend the landmark protections bipartisan majorities before him had put in place, he pledged to strengthen those safeguards to cope with emerging threats. And, as the country ground its way out of the worst economic downturn since World War II, the president rejected what he called the "false debate" between environmental protections and jobs.

"I do not buy the notion that we have to make a choice between having clean air and clean water, and growing this economy in a robust way," Obama said.

"When we put in place common sense rules to reduce air pollution, we create new jobs building and installing all sorts of pollution-control technology," he explained. "When we put in place new emission standards for our vehicles, we make sure that the cars of tomorrow are going to be built right here in the United States of America, that we're going to win that race," he said. "When we clean up our nation's waterways, we generate more tourists for our local communities. So what's good for the environment can also be good for our economy."

In the weeks that followed, the president also made clear that he would not turn his back on the promise of energy efficiency, wind, solar, and other renewable sources of power and the millions of American jobs that all can create. He would press forward, he vowed, with twenty-first century energy policies that are reducing our dangerous reliance on foreign oil.

THE QUESTION BEFORE US

Making our country more secure. Putting our people back to work. Creating a healthier future. Those are the stakes, for all Americans, in the great political contest over the fate of the environmental inheritance we've received from our forebears. It's our turn to safeguard those resources and pass them along to our children. The president can't do it alone, nor can either political party operating by itself. Standing up for our future is bipartisan work. The question before us—Republicans and Democrats alike—is the same one that has confronted generations of Americans past: will we rise, as a nation, to the challenge, or will we surrender to the power of corporate polluters and their allies on Capitol Hill?

"The citizens of the United States must effectively control the mighty commercial forces which they themselves have called into being," the great Republican conservationist, President Theodore Roosevelt, said in a 1910 speech in Osawatomie, Kansas. As clearly as any leader in our history, the flinty rough-rider understood what it meant to stand up to the influence of money in politics. His admonition on the subject still cuts like a beacon through the fog of our political discourse for everyone who cares about American democracy.

"It is necessary that laws should be passed to prohibit the use of corporate funds directly or indirectly for political purposes; it is still more necessary that such laws should be thoroughly enforced," Roosevelt said. "Corporate expenditures for political purposes," he said, "have supplied one of the principal sources of corruption in our political affairs."

Nowhere is that more apparent than in the political assault against our environment and health, a reckless and radical campaign that puts polluter profits first, and puts the rest of us at risk. The American people aren't asking Congress to eviscerate these essential safeguards that serve us so well, but someone else is.

With billions of dollars in annual profits in the balance, the oil, gas, and coal companies; operators of industrial incinerators, boilers, cement factories, and cement plants; as well as paper, chemicals, and other manufacturers, are investing heavily to advance their interests through our political system. After spending hundreds of millions of dollars on lobbyists who press their smokestack agenda in Washington, and then pumping millions more into the campaign war chests of the politicians who do their bidding, the biggest polluters in America are poised to spend record amounts on the November 6, 2012, elections, when the country will choose a president, a third of the U.S. Senate and the entire U.S. House of Representatives. In fact, the high-rolling influence peddling has already begun.

People and organizations associated with the oil and gas industry spent $31.8 million on campaign contributions during the 2010 congressional elections, with 77 percent of the money going to Republicans, according to the Center for Responsive Politics. The industry has already raised $13.6 million for the upcoming elections, with 88 percent going to Republicans so far. Coal mining companies spent $8.1 million in the 2010 elections, with 77 percent going to Republicans. And coal interests have already raised $2.7 million for the 2012 races, with 87 percent going to Republicans as of the middle of February 2012.

Large as they are, those sums pale in comparison to the spending already underway through the new so-called super PACs, or political action committees, formally known as "independent expenditure only committees."

In the 2010 *Citizens United* decision that infuriated heirs to Roosevelt's political conscience, the U.S. Supreme Court ruled 5–4 that corporations, unions and other groups may spend unlimited amounts of money to support a super PAC. The super PAC may then spend that money to run ads, host rallies, operate phone banks, distribute literature, and conduct various other activities to support or oppose a political candidate.

The court ruling allows those communications activities to take place without full or immediate disclosure of the donors, so the public often has no way of knowing who is behind the messaging. For deep-pocketed polluters who want to further tilt the political playing field in their favor, the court ruling was a gift of unimaginable proportions. Companies are now free to spend any amount of money they want to help get opponents of commonsense safeguards elected and to target for defeat those with the courage to stand up for our environment and health.

As of mid-March 2012, these new super PACs had already spent $75.3 million to boost or target political candidates, and they had another $55 million in their coffers, the Center for Responsive Politics reports. That's a lot of firepower, but it was just the beginning.

Industry has the right to lobby on behalf of its shareholders. And corporate money in politics isn't anything new. Opening the floodgates to unlimited funding directly from the corporate treasury, however, has vaulted American democracy into uncharted territory. Analysts aren't sure how it will impact the 2012 presidential and congressional elections. One thing is clear: it provides an arsenal of powerful new weapons for corporations in their effort to drown out the scattered and nominally funded voices of citizens who expect government to serve the people.

And it points to the urgent need for campaign finance reform, beginning with enhanced requirements for full disclosure.

IT'S OUR LEGACY TOO

If ever an issue spotlighted how clearly that matters, it's the future of our environment. Over the course of the past year, the country has seen what a difference a determined administration can make in the face of a sustained political assault. Despite the House attacks, 2011 was an extraordinary year for environmental gains.

The administration secured a historic agreement to roughly double the fuel mileage of cars and small trucks by 2025. New rules were put in place to reduce the toxic chemicals and soot belched into the air by industrial smokestacks. And the EPA is moving forward with plans to cut the carbon emissions from coal-fired power plants, while asserting itself in new ways to improve water quality and protect wildlife and wilderness lands.

The worst of the anti-environment measures passed by the House were held off in the Senate, where a thin Democratic majority either rejected outright or refused to act at all on various spending bill amendments and separate bills aimed at delaying, blocking, or watering down environmental safeguards. And sweeping legislation designed to make it difficult, if not impossible, to implement or enforce new environmental rules—the Transparency in Regulatory Analysis of Impacts On the Nation (TRAIN) Act, the Regulations from the Executive in Need of Scrutiny (REINS) Act, the Regulatory Flexibility Improvement Act, and the Regulatory Accountability Act—were all stuck in Senate committees as of March 2012 and seemed destined to go nowhere.

"They haven't succeeded," former EPA Administrator Christine Todd Whitman said of the House leaders' agenda to roll back the foundation of environmental protections. "What would really put it at risk is if Republicans get control of the Senate too, with people who are committed to this kind of ideology, or this kind of an approach to the environment," said Whitman, a career Republican who served as EPA chief under President George W. Bush. "If they were to win the presidency and the senate . . . and continue along this path, then I think it could be very, very bad for the country."

What would be best, she said, would be if Republicans could embrace their own party's long history of conservation and environmental stewardship, and, once more, the strong national consensus that supports all of that might be faithfully represented in Congress.

"It is time once again to put on battle gear; to charge out and remind the country that Republicans, whose party has an admirable record on environmental issues going back to Teddy Roosevelt, in fact still do care about asthma and allergies; about the effects on the young, the ill, and the elderly of particulates and hot polluted air; about hospital admissions and lung impairment," said William Reilly, another career Republican and former EPA Administrator to George H. W. Bush. "It's time to speak out," Reilly said in a November 2011 speech. "It's our legacy too."

For the moment, at least, observers and analysts hold out little hope for an environmental renaissance among the House majority GOP. Going into the 2012 elections, the candidates were too heavily influenced by the tea party movement, corporate lobbyists, and campaign donations from big polluters.

"They bought the ticket and they're already on the train, and that's not going to turn on a dime," said Jim DiPeso, spokesman for Republicans for Environmental Protection. "It would have to take some soul searching in the aftermath of political set backs."

That, of course, is what elections are for. Democracy grants voters the power to compel change. It does not preordain the outcome.

"Of all the questions which can come before this nation, short of the actual preservation of its existence in a great war, there is none which compares in importance with the great central tasks of leaving this land even a better land for our descendants than it is for us, and training them into a better race to inhabit the land and pass it on."

Those words ring as true today as when President Teddy Roosevelt spoke them in 1910, reminding Americans that "conservation is a great moral issue, for it involves the patriotic duty of insuring the safety and continuance of the nation." A few years later, a great war came and two decades after that an even greater one, both testing the safety and continuance of the nation. Through the coming together of the American people, and the leaders they freely elected, the nation survived those tests and many lesser ones since then.

This country's long history of rising to challenge and embracing change makes clear that we have more greatness yet in us than any of us might dare to imagine. We'll begin to shape that future the minute we gather once more around the common goals that have driven this country and bound us united from the dawning of the republic, when Americans first stood up as one and bent our collective spirit and uncommon will to building that better land.

ABOUT THE AUTHOR

Bob Deans is the author of the 2007 book *The River Where America Began: A Journey Along the James*. He coauthored the 2009 book, *Clean Energy Common Sense: An American Call to Action on Global Climate Change*, and the 2010 book *In Deep Water: The Anatomy of a Disaster, the Fate of the Gulf, and Ending our Oil Addiction*. A native of Richmond, Virginia, Deans spent twenty-five years as a correspondent for the *Atlanta Journal-Constitution* and other Cox newspapers before joining the Natural Resources Defense Council in 2009. He is a former president of the White House Correspondents Association and lives in Bethesda, Maryland, with his wife and their three children.